Amador

Amador

*...in which a father addresses his son
on questions of ethics—that is,
the options and values of
freedom—and attempts
to show him how to
have a good life...*

FERNANDO SAVATER

*Translated from the Spanish
by Alastair Reid*

A John Macrae Book

HENRY HOLT AND COMPANY
NEW YORK

Henry Holt and Company, Inc. / *Publishers since 1866*
115 West 18th Street / New York, New York 10011

Henry Holt ® is a registered trademark of
Henry Holt and Company, Inc.

First published in the United States in 1994
by Henry Holt and Company, Inc.
Published in Canada by Fitzhenry & Whiteside Ltd.
Originally published in Spain in 1991 by Editorial Ariel, S.A.,
under the title *Ética para Amador*.
Library of Congress Cataloging-in-Publication Data

Savater, Fernando.
[Etica para Amador.   English]
Amador : in which a father addresses his son on questions
of ethics . . . /Fernando Savater ; translated from
the Spanish by Alastair Reid.
p.   cm.
"A John Macrae book."
1. Ethics.   2. Fathers and sons.   3. Liberty.   I. Title.
BJ1144.S3512   1994   94-14218
170′.44—dc20   CIP

ISBN 0-8050-3271-1

Holt books are available for promotions and premiums; Contact:
Director, Special Markets.
First American Edition—1994
Designed by Brian Mulligan
Printed in U.S.A. on acid-free paper.∞

1   3   5   7   9   10   8   6   4   2

Permissions are listed on page 193.

To Sara, for her loving impatience with
Amador and with me

Author's Note

This book is simply a book, personal and subjective, like that which binds father and son, but in the same way universal, like the relation between fathers and sons, the most common of all. It has been thought and written with adolescents in mind—it probably has very little to say to their teachers. Its aim is not to turn out right-thinking (or wrong-thinking) citizens, but to help in developing, above all, free-thinking ones.

—Madrid
January 26, 1991

"Listen to *me*," said the Demon, as he placed his hand upon my head.

—EDGAR ALLAN POE, *Silence—A Fable*

Amador

Prologue

SOMETIMES, Amador, I have such an urge to tell you a great many things. I restrain myself, don't worry, for I have enough parts to play in just being your father without adding any extras in the guise of philosophy. I also know well that there is a limit to the patience of the young. Besides, I don't want to risk what happened to a Galician friend of mine who one fine day was gazing contentedly at the sea with his small son, when the little fellow said, dreamily, "Papa, I wish we could go out in a boat, you and Mama and I, out on the sea." My sentimental friend immediately felt a lump in his throat, just above the knot in his tie. "Of course, my boy, of course! We'll go whenever you like." "Then, when we're very far out," the little fellow went on, "I'll throw you both in the water to drown." Out of the poor father's being broke a sorrowful bellow. "But, my boy . . ." "Of course, Papa. Surely you must know that you parents give us children a lot of pain?" End of the first lesson.

If someone so small can be aware of it, I imagine that a fellow of over fifteen like you must know it only too well. So it is not my intention to give you any more excuses for killing your parents than those customary in families that get on well. On the other hand, they have always made me slightly uncomfortable, those fathers bent on being "best friend" to their sons. You should have friends of your own age, both male and female, certainly. With parents, teachers, and other adults it is possible at best to get along reasonably well, which is quite enough. But getting along reasonably well with adults includes at times wanting very much to drown them. Otherwise it's not worthwhile. If I were fifteen, I would be wary of all grownups who were too "understanding," all those who seemed as if they wanted to be younger than I, all those who were always telling me I was right. You know, the ones who are always coming up with "You young people are great," "I feel just as young as you," and stuff like that. Watch out for them! They're after something, with all that flattery. A father or a teacher is obliged to be a bit of a burden or he is useless. It's quite enough that you are young.

And so it has occurred to me to write down some of those things I wished to tell you from time to time, not knowing how to, not daring to. When a father starts playing philosopher, you have to look him in the eye, put on a somewhat attentive face, your mind fixed on the moment of liberation when you can rush off to television. But a book—a book you can read whenever you want, at odd moments, and you don't have to treat it with any respect. You can yawn while you are turning the pages, or laugh if you feel like it. You have complete freedom. Since most of what I am going to say to you has a great deal to do with freedom, it's much better that you read it than hear it in the form of a sermon. Now, you will have to give me some attention (about half of what you give to learning a new computer game) and have some *patience*, especially in the beginning chapters. Although I realize that it makes things somewhat more difficult, I didn't want to spare you from having to think *step by step*, or treat you as an idiot. I firmly believe—I don't know if you agree—that if you treat a person like an idiot, he will be more likely to become one.

What am I going to be talking to you about? About my life and yours, nothing more, nothing less; or, if you prefer, about what I do and what you are beginning to do. As for the first, what I do, I want finally to answer a question you once asked me out of the blue—you won't even remember—and that went unanswered then. You must have been about six, and you were spending the summer in Torrelodones. That afternoon, as often happened, I was tapping away without much enthusiasm on my Olivetti portable, shut up in my study in front of a photograph of the tail of an enormous whale, towering and glistening against a blue sea. I heard you playing with your cousins in the pool; I saw you racing through the garden. Forgive the sentimental aside, but I felt in myself a kind of sweat of happiness. Suddenly you came up to the open window and said to me, "Hello, there. What are you typing?" I gave some stupid answer—it was not the moment to set about explaining that I was trying to write a book on *ethics*. You were not the least interested in ethics, and you were not about to give me any more than three minutes of your attention. Possibly you just wanted to let me know that you were still there. As if I could ever have forgotten, then or now. Then you called to the others, and ran off. I went on typing, and only now, almost ten years later, have I decided to explain to you something about this curious thing, ethics, in which I am still immersed.

A couple of years later, also in our small paradise in Torrelodones, you told me about a dream you had had. Do you remember? You were in a field that was very dark, dark as night, when a terrible wind blew up. You clung to trees, to stones, but the hurricane tore you free, like the girl in *The Wizard of Oz*. When you were whirling through the air, into the unknown, you heard my voice ("I didn't see you but I knew it was you," you said) saying, "Keep your nerve! Have confidence!" You have no idea what a gift you gave me, telling me that strange nightmare. Never in a thousand years could I pay you back for the pride it gave me that afternoon to know that my voice could give you heart. And so, all that I am going to tell you in the following pages is not much more than repeating that one piece of advice over and over again: Keep your nerve! Have confidence! Not in me, not in wise men, even truly wise men, not in mayors, not in priests, not in the police. Not in gods, not in devils, not in machines, not in flags. Keep your nerve, have confidence in your own self. In your intelligence, which will enable you to become better than you presently are; in your love instincts, which will open you up to loving companions. This you can see is no mystery novel, where you have to read to the end to know who committed the crime. I'm in such a hurry that I begin in the prologue to tell you what is in the last chapter.

Since I am writing these chapters to you as father to son, I realize that my language and my examples have a distinct masculine cast. To correct that, I must make clear at this point that what I have to say throughout applies to men and women alike, for they face the same ethical dilemmas of freedom and choice, however different their circumstances.

Perhaps you suspect that I am trying to influence you, and in some sense you are not far wrong. Some anthropophagous peoples open, or opened, the craniums of their enemies to consume part of their brains, trying to ingest their wisdom, their myths, their courage. In this book, I am giving you a sense of what is in my mind, and also taking the chance to sample a little of yours. I don't know if you will get much sustenance from my brain—perhaps some flavor of the experience of someone who did not acquire it all from books. As for me, I want to enjoy a bite or two out of what you have in rich abundance: unused youth. I hope we both enjoy ourselves.

What About Ethics?

SOME BRANCHES OF KNOWLEDGE are studied out of a straightforward desire to know new things; others, to acquire a skill that will allow us to do something, to be useful; the majority, to help us find a job and earn a living. If we have neither the curiosity nor the need to know certain things, we can dispense with them without worrying. There is a wealth of interesting kinds of knowledge without which we can live perfectly well. For example, I regret to say I know nothing of astrophysics or cabinetmaking, in which others take pleasure, but my ignorance has not held me back so far. What I mean is that there are certain things we can learn or not, just as we decide. Since nobody can know everything, all we can do is choose, and humbly accept what we don't know. You can live without knowing astrophysics, or cabinetmaking, or football, even without knowing how to read or write. You live worse, of course, but you can live. Now, there are other things you have to know, because, as they say, they are your life. It's important to know, for example, that jumping from the sixth story is not good for your health, or that a diet of nails and prussic acid will not bring you long life. Nor is it wise to ignore a situation where every time you come across a certain neighbor, you fight with him. The consequences will sooner or later be very unpleasant. These small things are important. There are many ways of living; but there are ways that do not allow us to live.

Quite simply, among all kinds of knowing there is one at least that is essential to us: knowing that certain things *suit* us, while others do not.

Certain foods don't sit well with us, neither do certain kinds of behavior, certain attitudes. Clearly, I mean that they don't suit us if we want to go on living. If what one wants is to obliterate oneself right away, then drinking bleach would be fine, or else surrounding oneself with as many enemies as possible. But for the moment let us suppose that living is what we choose—let's leave on one side for now the considered choice of suicide. Now, certain things *suit* us, and these we usually call "good" things, for they make us feel *good;* on the other hand, other things that make us feel really *bad* we refer to as "bad" things. To know what suits us, that is, to distinguish between what is good for us and what is bad, is a sense we all try to acquire, all of us without exception, because of the advantages it brings us.

As I mentioned before there are things that are good for our health and bad for it. We have to know what we should eat. We have to know that fire sometimes warms and sometimes burns, just as water can sometimes quench our thirst and at other times drown us. Sometimes, however, things are not so simple. Certain drugs, for example, make us feel better, feel confident, but their continuous use would be bad for us. *In some respects*, they are good; in others, bad. They suit us and don't suit us at the same time. When it comes to human relations, these ambiguities turn up still more frequently. Lies are generally bad, for they destroy our faith in words—and we have to use words to live in human society—and they turn people into enemies. Yet at times it seems useful or beneficial to lie in order to gain some small advantage, or to do someone a favor. For example: Is it better to tell someone with an incurable cancer the truth or to deceive him in order to make his end better? Lies do not suit. They are bad, but sometimes they have good consequences. We have already said that picking a quarrel with others in the main does not suit at all; but can we stand by if a girl is attacked near us, not interfering just because we don't pick quarrels with others? Yet someone who always tells the truth, no matter what, must drive everyone mad; and anyone who barges in like Indiana Jones to rescue a girl who is being attacked might as likely end up with a broken head as go home whistling. Bad things sometimes seem to turn out more or less well, and good things sometimes look very bad. Such confusions!

Knowing how to live is not so easy, since there are various opposing points of view about what we ought to do. In mathematics or geography, there are bright people and ignorant people, but the bright people are almost always in agreement about fundamentals. In living, however, opinions are very far from unanimous. If you are after a life of excitement, you can apply yourself to Formula One motor racing, or to mountaineering, but if you prefer a safer and quieter life, it would be better to get your adventures from the video club on the corner. Some swear that the noblest thing is to live for others, while others demonstrate that it is more useful to contrive that others live for them. Some claim that what matters is making money and nothing else, whereas others argue that money without good health, free time, genuine affection, or peace of mind is worthless. Reputable doctors declare that giving up tobacco and alcohol is a sure way of extending one's life, to which smokers and drinkers reply that with such deprivations, of course life would seem much longer.

At first the only thing we can agree on is that we don't agree with everybody. But think. These differing opinions are in agreement on one thing: that whatever form our life takes will be the result, at least *in some part*, of what each of us wanted it to be. If our life were something completely determined, fixed and unchangeable, all these pronouncements would have no meaning at all. Nobody discusses whether stones fall up or fall down—they fall down, that's it. Beavers make dams in streams, and bees make combs with hexagonal cells. There are no beavers that try to make honeycomb cells, no bees that practice hydraulic engineering. In its natural medium, every animal seems to understand perfectly what is good for it and what is bad, no discussions, no doubts. There are no good animals and bad animals in nature, although possibly the fly considers the spider bad. But the spider has no choice in the matter.

Let me give you a dramatic example. You know about African termites, those white ants that build extraordinary nests several feet tall and hard as stone. Now, termites' bodies are soft, lacking the horn shell that protects other insects. The nest itself is their collective armor-plating against enemy ants better armed than they. But on occasion one of those nests breaks open: in a downpour, or when nudged by an elephant (elephants love to rub their flanks against termites' nests). Immediately, the worker-termites begin to reconstruct their damaged fortress at top speed. Huge enemy ants throw themselves into attack, and the soldier-termites come out to defend the tribe and to restrain the enemy. Since neither in size nor in weapons can they match the ants, they fling themselves on the attackers, trying to slow their progress, while the ferocious jaws of the assault troops chop them up. The worker-termites, working full out, manage to close the broken nest-wall, but in closing it they leave *outside* the poor heroic soldier-termites, who give up their lives for the others. Don't they at least deserve something like a medal? Surely it's correct to say they are *brave*.

Change of scene, but not of subject. In *The Iliad*, Homer tells the story of Hector, the Trojans' most celebrated warrior, feet planted firmly outside the walls of Troy, waiting for Achilles, the choleric champion of the Greeks, well aware that Achilles is much stronger than he and will probably kill him. He does it out of an obligation to defend his family and his fellow citizens against the ferocious assault. There is no question—Hector is a hero, a truly brave man. But is Hector heroic in the same way as the soldier-termites, whose sacrifices, made over and over again, no Homer has bothered to relate? Doesn't Hector after all do exactly what the anonymous termites do? Why is his bravery more authentic, more *complicated*, than that of the insects? What's the difference?

Quite simply, the difference lies in the fact that the soldier-termites fight and die because they *have* to: Like the spider that eats the fly, they have no choice in the matter. Hector, on the other hand, goes out to confront Achilles because he *wishes* to. The soldier-termites cannot desert or rebel, or call in sick so that others go in their place. They are essentially programmed by the natural order to complete their heroic mission. Hector's case is quite different. He could say that he was ill, that he had no wish to go up against someone stronger than he. His fellow citizens might call him a coward or a fraud, or they might ask him what other plan he had to deal with Achilles, but the point is that Hector can refuse to be a hero. However much pressure others bring to bear on him, he can always choose not to do what he is supposed to do. He is not *programmed* to be a hero—no man is. So his gesture has enormous merit, and Homer recounts it with epic emotion. We say that, as opposed to the termites, Hector was *free,* and for that we admire his courage.

And so we come to the essential word in all of this: *freedom.* Animals (to say nothing of minerals and plants) have no choice but to be as they are, and to do what they are programmed by nature to do. You can't criticize what they do, or applaud them for it, because *it is all that they know.* Of course, men too are to some extent programmed by nature. We are programmed to drink water, not bleach, and in spite of all the precautions we take, we have to die sooner or later. Similarly, though less loftily, our culture programs us: Our thinking is conditioned by the language we use to form it (a language that impresses itself on us from the outside, not one we have invented for our personal use), and we are educated into certain traditions, habits, forms of behavior, certain legends. In a word, what we develop from the cradle on are *loyalties*, loyalties to some things and not to others. That is quite a load, and it makes us somewhat predictable. Take Hector, whom we were discussing. His natural programming made him want protection, shelter, and the help of others, all of which he found, for better or worse, in Troy, his city. It was also natural for him to think affectionately of his wife Andromache, with whom he had shared many pleasures, and of his son, to whom he felt strong biological ties. Culturally, he felt himself to be part of Troy, sharing its language, its customs, and its traditions. Besides, since his childhood he had been brought up to be a good warrior in his city's service, and knew that cowardice was something abhorrent, unworthy of a man. If he betrayed his fellows, Hector knew that he would be despised and punished in one way or another. So wasn't he fairly well programmed to do what he did? And yet . . .

And yet Hector could have said, "Forget the whole business!" He could have dressed as a woman and escaped from Troy by night, he could have feigned illness or madness, he could have knelt before Achilles and offered his services as a guide for the invasion of Troy on its weakest flank. He could have turned to drink, or he could have invented a new religion that preached against fighting one's enemies, and recommended instead turning the other cheek. You might say that these various activities would be fairly *strange*, given who Hector was and the education he had had. But you must allow that they are at least *possible*, while a beaver making honeycombs or a soldier-termite deserting are not rare but utterly impossible. With people, you can never be sure; with animals and other natural beings, you can. For all our biological or cultural programming, we can always in the end choose something that is not in the program, or at least, not in everybody's program. We can say Yes or No, I want it, I don't want it. However much we are tumbled about by circumstance, we are never left with only one course to take; we have several.

I mentioned *freedom*. It's freedom I'm talking about. Freedom is what distinguishes us from the termites and the tides, from everything that obeys an unvarying necessity. It is true that we cannot do *just what we like*, but it is also true that we are not bound to do a single thing. And here we can set down two things about freedom:

ONE. We are not free to choose *what happens to us* (being born on a certain day, to certain parents, in a certain country; suffering from cancer or being annihilated in a car accident; being handsome or ugly), but we are *free to respond to what happens in such and such a way*. We can obey or rebel, we

can be prudent and tentative, vengeful or resigned, we can dress fashionably or wear a bear
costume, we can defend Troy or run away.

Two. Being free to *try* something has nothing
to do with bringing it off flawlessly. Freedom,
which means choosing among possibilities, has
nothing to do with omnipotence, which is getting
what you want however impossible it may seem.
Of course, the more ability we have, the better the
results we can obtain with our freedom. I am free
to want to climb Mount Everest, but given my
wretched physical condition and my total lack of
expertise in mountaineering, it is practically impossible that I do it. I am free to read or not to
read; since I learned to read as a child, reading
presents no difficulty if I decide to do it. There
are things that depend on my will (that's what
being free means); but not everything does, or
else I would be omnipotent. In the world there
are many other wills, many other necessities that I
do not control. If I am not aware of myself or the

world in which I live, my freedom will founder in the face of necessity over and over again. But— very important—that would not cause me to give up my freedom, although you might forgive me for doing so.

There are many forces in reality that limit our freedom, from hurricanes to dictators. But at the same time, our freedom is a force in the world, *our* force. If you speak to people, however, you will notice that most of them are much more aware of what limits their freedom than of the freedom itself. They will say to you: Freedom? What freedom are you talking about? How can we be free if our nourishment comes from television, if our governments deceive us and use us, if terrorists threaten us, if drugs enslave us, and if on top of that we don't have the money to buy a motorbike, which is really what we want? If you look a little more closely, you'll see that the people who speak like that seem to be complaining, but they are really very relieved to know they are not free.

They are thinking: "It doesn't really help. Since we are not free, anything that happens cannot be our fault." But I am convinced that nobody—*nobody!*—really believes they are not free, nobody accepts that they might be a piece of inexorable mechanism, like a watch or a termite. You might think that choosing certain things freely in certain circumstances could be difficult, like entering a burning house to save a child, or standing up to a bully, and that it's better to say there is no freedom so as not to have to realize that we freely choose the easiest way—that's to say, we wait for the firemen or lick the boot on our neck. But inside us something keeps saying, "If you had wanted. If you had really wanted . . ."

Whenever anything leads you to think that you might not be free, I suggest you apply the proof of a Roman philosopher. A long time ago, a Roman philosopher was talking with a friend who denied the liberty of man, and swore that men had no choice but to do what they did. The philosopher raised his stick and showered blows on his companion with all his strength. "Stop! That's enough, don't hit me anymore," cried the companion, and the philosopher, not pausing in his beating, explained. "You say I am not free, that I have no choice but to do what I do? Then don't waste your breath asking me to stop. I'm an automaton." Until his companion conceded the philosopher's freedom to leave off beating him, he did not stay his stick. Good proof, but you must only use it as a last resort.

To sum up: Unlike other beings, we humans can *invent* and *choose* the form our lives take. We can choose what seems good to us, that is, what suits us, as opposed to what seems bad or unsuitable. And since we can *invent* and *choose*, we can also *make mistakes*, something that does not happen to the beavers, the bees, and the termites. So it makes sense to apply ourselves to what we do, and to try to acquire enough of a sense of how to live to allow us to succeed. This knowing-how-to-live, the art of living, if you like, is what we call *ethics*. Be patient. We will talk more about it.

Selections for Further Reading

Were I to lay down my weighty helmet and lean my great bossed shield against the rampart, then go straight up to the flawless Achilles and promise to surrender Helen with all her precious belongings once and for all, everything that Paris had spirited away to Troy in his cavernous ships—for that was the start of all this strife—and just let the sons of Atreus reclaim it all; and if, what's more, I were simultaneously to guarantee a division of the entire wealth of our city, rendering half unto the Greeks; and I could then extract a solemn oath from our Trojan elders warranting that nothing should be held back but that we divide the whole lot right down the middle. . . . But why does my brave heart persist in debating these things even now?

—HOMER, *The Iliad*, 22.111–122

Freedom is not a philosophy, nor is it an idea—it is a stirring of conscience that causes us to utter, at certain moments, one of two monosyllables: Yes or No. In that instant, fleeting as a lightning flash, it shows the whole contradiction of human nature.

—OCTAVIO PAZ, *The Other Voice*

Man's life cannot "be lived" by repeating the pattern of his species; *he* must live. Man is the only animal that can be *bored*, who can be *discontented*, that can feel evicted from paradise.

—ERICH FROMM, *Man for Himself: An Inquiry into the Psychology of Ethics*

Rules, Habits, and Whims

TO REMIND YOU briefly of where we left off: It is clear that there are some things that suit our lives and others that do not, but it is not always clear which are the things that suit us. Although we cannot choose what happens to us, we can choose what to do about what happens. Modesty apart, our situation seems closer to Hector's than to that of the worthy termites. When we set out to do something, we do it because we *prefer* it over something else, or because we prefer doing it to not doing it. Does that mean that we always do what we want? Not quite: Sometimes circumstances make us decide between two options that we have not chosen, and there are even occasions in which we must choose although we would prefer not to.

Aristotle, one of the first philosophers to tackle these questions, came up with the following example. A boat is carrying important cargo from one port to another. In midpassage, it is caught in a tremendous storm. The only way of saving the boat and its crew, it seems, is to jettison the cargo, which, although valuable, is a burden. The captain faces the following problem: Should he jettison the cargo or risk riding out the storm with it in the hold in the hope that the weather will improve and the boat hold out? If he abandons his cargo, it will of course be because he prefers that to taking the risk, but it would be unfair to say that he *wants* to abandon it. What he really wants is to arrive in port with boat, crew, and cargo intact; that is what would best *suit* him. Given the stormy circumstances, however, he prefers saving his own life and the lives of his crew to saving his cargo, however valuable it may be. If only the wretched storm had not blown up! But the storm is not a matter of choice, but something given, something that *happens*, like it or not. What he can choose, on the other hand, is how he acts in the face of danger. If he abandons the cargo, he does it because he wants to, while simultaneously not wanting to. He wants to live, to save himself and the men who depend on him, to save his boat; he does not want to lose the cargo and the profit it stands for, for which reason he will abandon it only with the greatest reluctance. He would unquestionably prefer not to be in the critical situation of having to choose between losing his worldly goods and losing his life. There is no other choice, however, and he must decide. He will choose the course he prefers, the one that best suits him. We could say that he is free because he cannot be otherwise, free to choose in circumstances he did not elect to confront.

Almost always, when we are faced with choosing what to do in difficult or important situations, we find ourselves in the same boat as Aristotle's captain. Our choices are not always so brutal, however. Circumstances are much less troubled at times, and if I persist in coming up with loaded examples, you can resist them, like the student pilot whose flying instructor asked him, "You're in a plane, a storm blows up, your motor gives out, what do you do?" "Go on the other motor," the student answers. "Very well, but another storm hits and takes out that motor. What then?" "I'd go on the other motor," and so on. "Wait a minute," said the instructor. "Where are you getting all those motors?" "From the same place that you are getting all those storms," the student answered, unperturbed. But let us not torment ourselves over torments. Let's see what happens in fine weather.

We do not in general spend our lives attending only to what it suits us to do or not to do. Fortunately, we are not usually so beset by life as the captain of the boat. If we are honest, we have to concede that we perform most acts almost automatically, without giving them very much attention. Think about what you've done this morning. The alarm went off indecently early, and instead of hurling it against the wall as you wanted, you turned it off. You stayed in bed briefly, trying to savor the last luxurious moments, then you thought of the time and the impatient school bus and you rose with a certain resignation. I know you don't like brushing your teeth, but since I have always insisted strongly, you brushed between yawns. You showered almost without realizing it, since showering is a matter of pure daily routine. Then you had your usual tea and milk, toast and butter; then, into the street. While you walked to the bus stop with math problems on your mind, you distractedly kicked at an empty soda can. Then the bus, school, your day.

Frankly, I doubt that any one of these acts has

stirred up much deliberation in you: Do I get up
or don't I? Do I shower or not? To breakfast or
not to breakfast, that is the question! The di-
lemma of the poor captain about to founder, trying to decide on the spur of the moment whether
or not to ditch his cargo, does not seem at all like
the morning decisions you sleepwalked through.
You acted unthinkingly, almost by instinct—it's
easier like that, isn't it? At times wondering too
much about what we are going to do can paralyze
us. It's like learning to walk: If you keep looking
at your feet and saying, "Now the right, next the
left," you will end up falling down or unable to
move. But I would like to ask you now, in retro-
spect, what you didn't ask yourself this morning:
Why did I do what I did? Why this particular
movement, why not its opposite, or some other?

I imagine that such questions must irritate you,
as to why you have to get up at seven-thirty, brush
your teeth, and go to school, particularly coming
from me, since I am the one who pushes you into

what you do and who keeps pestering you in a thousand ways with threats and promises. If you made a practice of staying in bed, imagine the row! Now, some things, like showering or having breakfast, you do on your own, since they go with getting up. In the same way, you put on pants instead of going out in your shorts, although it is hot outside. As for taking the bus, it's the only way of arriving in time, for the school is too far for you to walk, and I am not in a position to pay for a taxi to deliver you and pick you up every day. And kicking the tin can? You do that just because you feel like it.

Let's look at the different motives behind your morning activities. You understand what is meant by a motive in this context: It is the reason you have, or think you have, for doing anything, the most acceptable explanation for your actions when you think about them, the answer you come up with to the question "Why am I doing this?" Well, one kind of motive you recognize is that I tell you to do this or that. Motives of this kind we will call *rules*. In other cases, your motive is that you have always done certain things in the same way, almost without thinking, or that you see around you everyone else doing things in ways they are used to; that set of motives we will call *habits*. In other cases, as when you kicked the can, the motive seems to be a lack of motive—just something you felt like doing, something you wanted to do. Supposing we call these actions *whims*? Let us put aside motives that are no more than *functional*, that is, those that lead you to do certain things in order to accomplish something, pure and simple, like going downstairs to get to the street instead of jumping out the window, or taking the bus to get to school, or using a cup for tea, and so on.

We'll confine ourselves to the first three motives: rules, habits, and whims. Each one *directs* your actions in one way or another, and more or less reveals your preference for doing one thing as opposed to many other things you might do. The first question that occurs to me is this: Just how, and just how strongly, does each impulse drive you to act? Because they don't all have the same force on every occasion. Getting up to go to school is more of an obligation than brushing your teeth or showering, and a good bit more than kicking a can; and yet putting on your pants is as much of an obligation as going to school, isn't it? What I mean is that each kind of motive has its own importance, which you come to understand. Orders or rules, for example, gain their force in part from the *fear* that you may have of the terrible reprisals I may visit on you if you don't obey me; but also, I imagine, from the affection and trust you have for me, which makes you aware that what I oblige you to do is to protect you and help you along, or, to use an old expression that must make you wince, *for your own good*. Also, of course, because you expect some kind of reward if you do what you are supposed to do: a payment, or a gift. Habits, on the other hand, arise more from the usefulness of following a routine on certain occasions, and also from your wish not to be different from others. They arise, that is, from the pressure of others. Habits also obey certain kinds of rules: think of fashions. Think of the number of jackets, shoes, and caps you have just because they are in fashion among your friends and you don't want to be out of step!

Rules and habits have one thing in common: They come *from the outside*, and they impose themselves on you without asking your permission. Whims, on the other hand, come from the inside. They spring up spontaneously—nobody orders them, nor are you trying to imitate others. If I were to ask you when you feel most free, obeying rules, following habits, or acting on whim, I imagine you would plump for your whim, because it is more yours, and does not depend on others. Of course you will: Perhaps your whim appeals to you because you are imitating someone else, or perhaps it arises from a rule, but contrari-wise, from an urge to disobey which would not have occurred to you without the rule. Let us leave the matter here for now—this is confusion enough for one day.

Before we finish, however, let us go back once more to Aristotle's Greek boat in the storm. When we left him, the captain was facing the critical choice of dumping his cargo overboard to keep his ship from foundering. Now, his orders are to deliver his cargo to port, and it is not customary to throw cargo into the sea; and it would not help if he were to act on whim, given his predicament. Will he follow orders even at the risk of losing his life and the lives of his crew? Is he more afraid of the anger of his masters than that of the raging sea? Normally, it is quite enough to obey orders, but sometimes it is wiser to question the advisability of doing so. After all, the captain is not like the termites, who must fulfill their kamikaze destiny, since they have no choice but to obey the dictates of their own nature.

If rules are not enough to resolve a situation, habits are still less help. Habits are useful for routine, everyday matters, but a storm at sea is not a routine matter. Every morning, you dress religiously, but if a fire broke out and left you no time, you wouldn't feel at all at fault. When the great earthquake hit Mexico City years ago, a friend of mine watched a tall building collapse, and went immediately to help with the rescue work. He tried to free one of the victims, who seemed inexplicably reluctant to be rescued from the rubble and finally said, "You see, I don't have anything on." Such conformity seems a bit morbid, don't you think? We can suppose that our Greek captain was a practical man, and that the obligation to save his cargo would not be enough to affect his behavior in the face of danger. Even

though in the majority of cases it would be customary to abandon the cargo, he would not neces-
sarily do so. Truly grave situations call for
invention, not a simple following of habit or con-
vention.

In such a situation, it is no more appropriate to
fall back on whim. If I told you that the captain
ditched his cargo not because he thought it prudent to do so but on a hunch (or if he kept it in
the hold on a similar whim) what would you say?
Let me answer: You'd say he was a bit crazy. To
risk lives or fortunes from nothing more than
caprice smacks of irresponsibility, and if it endan-
gers the lives and fortunes of others, it deserves to
be judged even more harshly. How could someone irresponsible and capricious have come to be
in a position of command? In stormy circumstances, a sane person puts all caprice behind him
and wants only to do what is most appropriate, or
rather, most rational.

The problem then is one of *function*, of finding the best way to arrive in port safe and sound. Let us suppose that the captain reaches the conclusion that safety lies in dumping overboard a certain amount of *weight*, be it cargo or crew. He could then try to convince four or five of the more expendable of his sailors to go overboard, so giving him a better chance of saving his profitable cargo. From a functional point of view, that might be the best way of saving both lives and profits. Such a resolution, however, seems repugnant to me, and also, I imagine, to you. Is this because *rules* tell me that such things are not done, or because I am not in the *habit* of doing such things, or simply because, as a creature of *whim*, it doesn't appeal to me to behave in such a way?

Forgive me for leaving you in a suspense almost worthy of Hitchcock, but I am not going to tell

you what our vacillating captain did in the end.
Let's hope he guessed right and caught a good
wind into port. In truth, when I think of him, I
realize that we are all in the same boat. For now,
let us stay with the questions, and hope that favorable winds will take us on to the next chapter,
where we will find them again and try to answer
them.

Selections for Further Reading

We may claim full credit for our own excellence
—and likewise our meanness. If we are answerable for the commission of an act, so then are
we answerable for its omission; it is for ourselves
alone to determine whether we answer No or
Yes. Just as the performance of a worthy deed
redounds to our credit, so likewise must its omission shroud us in shame; if refraining from an

action were the better choice, so likewise would it be shameful to undertake it.

—ARISTOTLE, *Nichomachean Ethics*

In the art of living, *man is both the artist and the object of his art;* he is the sculptor *and* the marble; the physician *and* the patient.

—ERICH FROMM, *Man for Himself: An Inquiry into the Psychology of Ethics*

Four moral positions are open to us:

1. The Philosophical: Do good for the sake of the good, out of respect for the law.

2. The Religious: Do good because it is the will of God, out of love of God.

3. The Humanistic: Do good because your well-being demands it, out of respect for yourself.

4. The Political: Do good because it serves the society of which you are a part, out of love for your fellow men and consideration for yourself.

—GEORG CHRISTOPH LICHTENBERG,
Aphorisms

The objective is to live a full life, not just a long one: Survival into old age requires only good luck, whereas living *enough* demands character. Indeed, a life is long only when it has been fully lived; its fulfilment comes only when the mind has learned to supply its own bounty and to empower itself from within.

—SENECA, *Letters to Lucilius*

Do What
You Want

WE WERE SAYING before that most of the things we do, we do because we are told to —by our parents when we are young, by our superiors and by law when we are older—because we become accustomed to doing things in that way. Sometimes others impose their routine on us by example and pressure—fear of ridicule, censure, or gossip, or else our longing to be accepted by the group—and sometimes we impose it on ourselves. It is a way of getting what we want (like catching the bus to go to school) or simply of exercising our whim, of deciding to do things a certain way. But on important occasions, or when we are taking what we are doing with the utmost seriousness, all these reasons for acting are unsatisfactory. They do not turn you on, as they say.

When you have to present yourself on the battlefield under the walls of Troy, defying Achilles, as Hector did, or when you have to decide between throwing the cargo overboard to save the crew or throwing some of the crew overboard to save the cargo, neither instructions nor customs are enough, nor is it a question of whim. The occasions need not be as extreme—for example, should I vote for a politician whom I think good for the country, even if it means I have to pay higher taxes, or should I support the one who lets me fill my pockets, and hang the rest? The commandant of a Nazi concentration camp, accused of murdering Jews, tried to excuse himself by saying he was "following orders." That's no justification to me. In certain countries it is the practice not to rent apartments to black people because of their color, or to homosexuals because of their sexual proclivities. Although this is common, such discrimination cannot ever be acceptable to me. The impulse to spend some days at the beach is understandable, but if you have a small baby in your charge and abandon it for a beach weekend, that would have no appeal: It would be criminal. Don't you agree?

All this has to do with *freedom*, which is what *ethics* is about. Freedom is being able to say Yes or No; I'll do it or I won't do it, whatever my superiors say, whatever anybody says. It suits me and I want it. That other does not suit me so I don't want it. Freedom is *deciding;* but it is also, don't forget, *realizing* what you are deciding. It's exactly the opposite of being carried away by something. To keep yourself from being carried away, you must think, think at least twice, about what you are going to do. Yes, twice. I'm sorry if that's hard. The first time you think about what you are going to do, you try to answer the question "Why am I doing this?" It's what we have just talked about. I'm doing it because they told me to, because it's the accepted practice; I'm doing it just because I feel like it. But if you think a second time, it all changes. I'm doing it because they tell me to, but why am I obeying? Fear of punishment? Hope of a reward? Am I not then *enslaved* to those who command me? If I obey because the one who gave the orders knows more than I do, shouldn't I then learn enough to decide for myself? And if they order things that don't suit, like the Nazi commandant who was ordered to exterminate Jews in a concentration camp? Could something not be "bad," for me, unsuitable, however much I am directed to do it, and something else "good" and suitable even if no one at all orders me to do it?

The same happens with habits and customs. If I think of what I am doing only once, perhaps I will be satisfied with a reply like "It's the custom!" But why must I always do what is usually

done (or what I usually do)? It's not as if I were a
slave of those around me, good friends though
they may be, or of what I did yesterday, or the day
before, or a month ago. If I live among people
who customarily discriminate against black people, and if that is utterly unacceptable to me, why
do I have to do as they do? If I have developed
the habit of borrowing money and never paying it
back, feeling ashamed on every occasion, why
can't I change my habits and begin at once to be
more responsible? Maybe some of my habits
don't suit me very well, however used to them I
am. And when I question some of my impulses a
second time, I see the same thing. Often I have an
urge to do things that immediately turn in my
disfavor, things I later regret. In unimportant matters, sudden impulses may be acceptable, but in
serious matters, to allow myself to be carried away
by them, without thinking whether they suit me or
don't suit me, can be very unwise, even danger-

ous. To run a red light can be thrilling once or twice, but if I make a habit of it, will I live very long?

It would be silly to go against all rules and all customs, silly to ignore all impulses, for sometimes they suit very well, with pleasant results. *But an action is never good just because it obeys a rule, a custom, or an impulse.* To find out if something really suits me or not, I have to go more deeply into what I am doing, discuss it with myself. For a small child, immature and with little experience of life or reality, rules, routines, and whims are sufficient, because as small children we are still in the hands of others who watch out for us. Later, we turn adult, which is to say that we can to some extent invent our own lives, not simply live lives that others have invented for us. Naturally we can't invent everything, for we don't live alone, and many things impose themselves on us, whether we like it or not. But among the rules that are applied to us, among the habits and customs that surround us and that we create, among the sudden impulses that occur to us, we will have to learn to choose for ourselves. To be people and not sheep (may sheep forgive me), we must think twice about what we do, even three and four times, on occasions where it seems appropriate.

The word "moral" is etymologically bound up with customs—the Latin word *mores*—and also with rules. Most moral precepts have the same form: You must do this, you must never think of doing this other. There are, however, accepted customs and rules that can be bad or "immoral," however firm they appear. If we want to find what is truly moral, if we really want to put to good use the freedom we have (and in just such an apprenticeship lie the "morals" or the "ethics" we are speaking of here), it is best to separate ourselves from rules, customs, habits, and sudden whims. The first thing to make clear is that the ethical position of a free human being has nothing whatever to do with punishments or rewards given out

by others—authorities human or divine, it
doesn't matter. Someone who does no more than
stay clear of punishment or go after the rewards
handed out by others according to their own
lights, is no more than a poor slave. The carrot
and the stick may serve to direct a child's behavior, but can only seem woeful to a sentient being.
We have to think otherwise. But first, a termino-
logical clarification. Although I keep using the
words "morals" and "ethics" as if they were
equivalents, from a technical point of view they
refer to different things. "Morals" denotes the
cluster of standards of behavior that you, I, and
most of those around us generally accept as valid.
"Ethics" refers to our reflections as to *why* we
consider them worthwhile, and to our consideration of the moralities of different groups and
other people. But—may the academy forgive me!
—I will go on using the two words as one, in
talking of the *art of living*.

I remind you that the words "good" and "bad"

apply not only to moral attitudes, not even just to people. Maradona and Butragueno are said to be very good soccer players, although this assessment has nothing to do with whether they help their neighbors or always tell the truth. They are good quite simply as sportsmen, without our going into their private lives. We can also say that a particular motorbike is good without giving the impression that it is a Santa Teresa among motorbikes, just that it runs beautifully, and does everything you can ask of a motorbike. In the case of soccer players and motorbikes, what is "good," what suits, is clear enough. If I ask you, I'm sure that you can explain to me the qualities that make someone outstanding in the field of sport. And so I say, why can we not try in the same way to define what is necessary to make a man good? Would that not resolve all the problems we are raising?

It is not, however, easy. About good soccer players, good motorbikes, good racehorses, the majority of people usually agree, but when it's a question of determining whether someone is in general good or bad as a human being, opinions vary tremendously. Take, for example, the case of a schoolgirl like Purita: At home, she is well behaved and obedient, and her mother is delighted with her, but in class everyone hates her for being a gossip and a troublemaker. Sometimes calling someone "good" does not mean anything good, as when we say "So-and-so is so *good*, poor thing!" The Spanish poet Antonio Machado was aware of this ambiguity, and in his poetic autobiography he wrote, "I am good, in the good sense of the word." In many cases, to call someone "good" implies a mere docility, a tendency to agree and give no trouble. A "good" person is one who changes the records or CDs while the others dance, things like that.

To some, to be good means to be resigned, patient; but others think of a good person as one who is go-ahead, original, who says what he thinks when he wants, no matter if he gives offense. In countries like South Africa, for example, some will consider good those blacks who do not give trouble and accept apartheid, while others will apply the word only to followers of Nelson Mandela. And do you know why it is not at all easy to say when a human being is good or not? *Because we don't know what human beings are for.* A soccer player is good at playing soccer in a way that helps his team to win and score goals against the opposition; a good motorbike carries us swiftly, stably, reliably. We know when a specialist or an instrument *functions* well through an idea we have of what they are meant to do and what is expected of them. But if we take human beings in general, things become more complicated. As human beings we are resigned at times and rebellious at others, sometimes inventive, sometimes obedient, sometimes generous and sometimes wary of the future. Virtue is not easy to pin down either. For a soccer player to score cleanly against his opponents is always good, but telling the truth can very well not be. Would you call good someone who delivers a cruel truth to a person about to die or someone who reveals the hiding place of a would-be victim to a murderer? Functions and instruments meet some norms of usefulness set from outside that are clear enough: If they do what they're meant to do, good; if not, bad, out with them. Nothing else is asked of them. Nobody requires an athlete, as such, to be charitable or truthful; nobody requires a motorbike, as a good motorbike, to hammer in nails. But in the case of human beings, nothing is as clear-cut, because there is not a single rule about what makes a human being good, nor are we instruments that do anything in particular.

There are many ways of being a good man (or a good woman), and opinions on human behavior are likely to vary according to circumstance. So sometimes we say of people that they are good "in their way." We concede that there are many ways of being good and that the question depends much on circumstances. So you can see that it is not easy to decide *from outside* who is good or who is bad, who does what suits, who not. You would have to study not only all the circumstances in each case but also the *intentions* of everyone. It could happen that someone had pretended to do something bad that had apparently come out well quite indirectly. And would we not call "good" someone who does something good and suitable through a pure fluke? Or the other way round: Anyone, however well disposed to the world, could cause a disaster and be looked on as a monster without being at all to blame.

If we have established that neither rules nor customs nor impulses are enough to guide us ethically, and that there is no clear set of rules that teaches a man to be good and always act as such, how can we make ethical sense? I'm going to answer with something that will certainly surprise and perhaps scandalize you. A most engaging

French writer of the sixteenth century, François Rabelais, recounted in one of his novels the adventures of the giant Gargantua and his son Pantagruel. I could go on at length about that book but I would prefer you to read it for yourself, sooner or later. I will tell you of only one occasion, when Gargantua decides to found a more-or-less religious order and set it up in an abbey, the Abbey of Theleme, over the door of which is written this single legend: DO WHAT YOU WANT. And all the inhabitants of that blessed house do exactly that, they do what they want. What if I tell you that over the door of ethics could be written exactly the same thing: DO WHAT YOU WANT. You might be indignant. So that's our moral? The conclusion we arrive at? Think what would happen if everybody in the world did just what they wanted. For that we have spent all this time and mulled all this over? Wait, wait! Give me another chance, please, another chapter. . . .

Selections for
Further Reading

All their life was laid out not by laws, statutes, or
rules but according to their will and free choice.
They got up out of bed when they saw fit, drank,
ate, worked, slept when they came to feel like
doing so; no one woke them, no one forced them
either to drink or to eat or to do anything else
whatsoever. Gargantua had arranged it so. The
only rule of their Order was this:

DO WHAT YOU WANT

Reasonable enough, for people who are free,
wellborn, and well-educated, when they are
dealing with honorable people, feel naturally the
impulse and stimulus to flee from vice, and
welcome virtue. That is what they refer to as
honor.

But when the same people are oppressed and
constrained, they tend to rebel and throw off the

yoke that confines them. All of us always lean
toward the forbidden and crave what is denied us.
—RABELAIS, *Gargantua and Pantagruel*

Humanistic ethics, in contrast to authoritarian
ethics, may likewise be distinguished by formal
and material criteria. *Formally,* it is based on the
principle that only man himself can determine the
criterion for virtue and sin, and not an authority
transcending him. *Materially,* it is based on the
principle that "good" is what is good for man and
"evil" what is detrimental to man; *the sole criterion
of ethical value being man's welfare.*
—ERICH FROMM, *Man for Himself: An Inquiry
into the Psychology of Ethics*

Though reason, when fully assisted and
improved, be sufficient to instruct us in the
pernicious or useful tendency of qualities and
actions, it is not alone sufficient to produce any
moral blame or approbation. Utility is only a

tendency to a certain end, and were the end totally indifferent to us, we should feel the same indifference toward the means. It is a requisite a *sentiment* should here display itself, in order to give a preference to the useful above the pernicious tendencies. This sentiment can be no other than a feeling for the happiness of mankind, and a resentment for their misery, since these are the different ends which virtue and vice have a tendency to promote. Here therefore *reason* instructs us in the several tendencies of actions, and *humanity* makes a distinction in favor of those which are useful and beneficial.

—DAVID HUME, *An Enquiry Concerning the Principles of Morals*

Give Yourself
a Good Life

I N PROPOSING "Do what you want" as a corner-
stone of the ethics we are struggling to clarify,
what am I trying to say to you? Quite simply, that
you have to turn your back on orders and habits,
on rewards and punishments, on anything that
tries to direct you from the outside, and that you
must confront all matters as yourself, with the
inner authority of your will. Don't ask anyone
else what you should do with your life; ask yourself. If you want to know how best to use your
freedom, don't lose it for a start by subjecting
yourself to serving someone else, or other people,
however good, wise, or respectable they may be.

Now, since you are intelligent, you must realize that there is a certain contradiction here. If I
say to you "Do what you want," it seems as if I
am giving you an order, namely, "Do this and not
that," even though I am ordering you to act
freely. If you look at it closely, the order is quite
complex. If you obey it, you are disobeying it
(since you are not doing what *you* want, but what
I want, and what I tell you to do); if you disobey,
you are obeying it (since you are doing what you
want instead of what I tell you to do—but that is
just what I am telling you to do!). Believe me, I'm
not trying to set you a puzzle like those under
"Pastimes" in the newspapers. Although I try to
tell you all this lightly so that it does not become
unnecessarily boring, the matter is most serious:
It's not a question of *passing* the time, it's about
living it well. The apparent contradiction inherent
in "Do what you want" is only a reflection of the
essential paradox of freedom: that we are not free
not to be free, that we have no choice but to be

free. And if you tell me that you are weary of
freedom, and don't want to go on being free? Or
if you decide to offer yourself as a slave to the
highest bidder or swear eternal obedience to some
tyrant or other? You will do it because you
choose to, exercising your freedom; although you
obey someone else or let yourself be carried along
by the masses, you will be doing what you want to
do. You will not have given up choice—you will
have chosen not to choose for yourself. The
French philosopher Jean-Paul Sartre declared that
"we are condemned to freedom." From that sen-
tence there is no exemption.

So, my "Do what you want" is nothing more
than a way of telling you to take very seriously the
question of your own freedom. Nobody can excuse or exempt you from the creative responsibility of choosing your own path. Don't go asking
yourself gloomily if all this fuss about freedom is
worth the trouble, for, like it or not, you are free,
like it or not, you have to want. Although you

may say that you're not interested in such hair-splitting, that I should leave you in peace, you will still be choosing—choosing not to know, wanting me to leave you in peace, although with some touch of cowardice. But let's not confuse "Do what you want" with the whim we spoke of earlier. It is one thing to do what you want and another, quite distinct, to do the first thing that appeals to you. I'm not saying that there are not occasions when a simple wanting is enough: for example, in choosing what you want to eat in a restaurant. Luckily, you have a good digestion and are not worried about your weight, so go ahead, order what appeals to you. But watch out, sometimes that urge can turn against you. Here's an example:

I don't know whether you have read much in the Bible. It is full of interesting things and you don't have to be particularly religious to appreciate it. The first book, Genesis, tells the story of Esau and Jacob, the sons of Isaac. They were twin brothers, but Esau was the firstborn, which meant he was his father's heir—in those days, the firstborn inherited all the possessions and privileges of the father. Esau loved hunting and adventure, while Jacob preferred to stay home, occasionally preparing enticing dishes. One day, Esau returned from the chase exhausted and hungry. Jacob had prepared an appetizing lentil stew, and when his brother smelled it cooking, his mouth watered. He wanted to eat at once and asked Jacob to serve it to him. His brother agreed, but added that he would not feed him for nothing, and asked in exchange for his birthright, his right of inheritance. Esau thought, "What I crave now is the lentil stew. What I inherit from my father will come much later. I might even die before him, who knows!" And he agreed to exchange his future inheritance for an immediate serving of the succulent stew. Those lentils must have smelled amazingly good! Needless to say, later, with a full stomach, Esau had second thoughts about the bad arrangement he had made, which would later cause such difficulties between the brothers (with all due respect, it has always seemed to me that Jacob was a very calculating fellow). If you want to know the rest of the story, read Genesis; but I have told you enough to underline what interests us here.

Since you are somewhat contrary, it would not surprise me if you were to try to use this story to contradict what I am saying. "Didn't you tell me how advisable it is to 'Do what you want'? Well, look: Esau wanted stew, he made a bargain in order to get it, and ended up with no inheritance. Some bargain!" Very well. But was the stew what Esau *really* wanted, or just what appealed to him at that moment? After all, being the firstborn was a valuable asset in those days, certainly compared to a lentil stew. Logical to conclude that what Esau really wanted was his inheritance, which would improve his lot considerably in the not-so-distant future. Of course, he also wanted to eat the stew, but if he had taken the trouble to think a little, he would have realized that that urge was secondary and could wait a little, and not destroy his chances of inheritance. At times, we want contradictory things, things that conflict. It is important to be able to set priorities and to arrange a certain hierarchy of what is immediately desirable and what we want in the long run. If you disagree, ask Esau.

In the biblical story, there is an important detail. What causes Esau to choose the stew in the present moment and renounce his future inheritance is the shadow of death or, if you prefer, the shadow that is cast by the brevity of human life. "Since I know I'm going to die in the long run, possibly even before my father, why bother thinking about what is best for me? At this moment I crave lentil stew and tomorrow I may be dead, so bring on the lentils and have done!" From fear of death, Esau decides to live as if he were already dead. It seems as if the certainty of death led him to believe that life is not worth the trouble, that it doesn't matter. But what makes it not matter is not life, but death. Esau lives as if for him there is no other reality than the aroma of lentil stew in his nostrils, no yesterday, no tomorrow. What is more, our lives consist of relationships with others—we are fathers, sons, brothers, friends or enemies, heirs or landowners—but Esau decides that lentils (a *thing,* not a *person*) are more important to him than those connections to other people that make him who he is. Now, a question: Does Esau really get what he wants, or has death hypnotized him, paralyzing and upsetting his love and his will?

Let us leave Esau with his culinary whims and his family crises. Let's get back to your case, which is the one that interests us. If I tell you to do what you want, the first and most opportune thing for you to do is to stop and think deeply about what it is that you want. Many things appeal to you, no question, often even contradictory

things. You would like to have a motorbike but
you don't want to take a spill on the highway; you
want to have friends but you don't want to lose
your independence; you'd like to have money but
you don't want to take advantage of others to get
it; you want to know things and so you realize
that you have to study, but you also want to have
fun; you want me not to pester you, to give you
room to be, but you also want me to be there to
help you when you need help. If you had to sum
all this up, you'd say, "Look, what I really want is
to give myself a good life." Bravo, first prize!
That's just what I would tell you. When I say
"Do what you want," what I am basically trying
to urge on you is that you dare to go for a good
life. Don't pay attention to pessimists or fanatics.
Ethics is nothing more than the rational attempt
to discover how to live better. If taking an interest
in ethics is at all worthwhile, it is because a good
life pleases us. Only those born into slavery or so

terrified by death that nothing matters give themselves up to lentils and get by as best they can.

You want to go for a good life? Splendid. But you also want that good life to be not the good life of a cauliflower or a beetle, but a good *human* life. That is what suits you, I think. I'm sure you would not give it up for anything. Being human, as we have seen, consists mainly in having relations with other human beings. If you had a huge amount of money, a house more sumptuous than a palace from *A Thousand and One Nights*, the best clothes, the finest of food (plenty of lentils!), the most sophisticated gadgets, all that at the cost of never seeing or never being seen by another human being, would you be content? How long could you live without going mad? Surely it is the height of madness to want things at the expense of relations with other people? The advantage of all these things lies precisely in the fact that they allow you—or seem to allow you—to enjoy bet-

ter relations with others. Money is used to dazzle
other people, even to buy them; clothes are to
please them or make them envious; the big house,
the best wines, same thing; and the gadgets—
video and television are to see them better,
compact discs to hear them better, and so on.
Very few things keep their charm in solitude;
and if the solitude is absolute and complete,
everything turns irretrievably to ashes. A good
human life is a good life *among other human beings.*
If otherwise, it may be life, but it will be neither
good nor human. Do you see what I am getting at?

Things may be good and useful, animals (at
least some) may be amiable, but we want to be
human beings, not mere instruments or creatures,
and we want also to be treated as humans, because
what we call humanity depends in good measure
on how we treat one another. To explain: A peach
grows as a peach, a leopard arrives in the world as
a leopard, but a man is not born a man, nor will

he become one without the help of others. Why? Because a person is not simply a biological reality, a natural object like a peach or a leopard, but is also a cultural reality. Humanity demands a cultural apprenticeship, and demands for a start the foundation of all culture, and of so much of our humanity, namely, language. The world we humans live in is a linguistic world, a reality made up of symbols and laws without which we would not only be incapable of communi among ourselves but also unable to re meaning of everything around us. But n earns to speak by himself (as he could learn to eat or make water) because language is not a natural biological function (although it clearly is based in our biological condition). It is a cultural creation that we inherit and learn from other people.

So speaking and listening to other people is to treat them as people, at least to grant them the beginnings of humanity. A first step, of course, because the culture within which we become human originates from language but is not simply language. There are other ways of showing that we recognize one another as human—forms of respect and courtesy that we show to others. We all wish to be treated in a certain way, and if we are not, we complain. The process of humanization (what turns us into what we wish to be, that is, human beings) is a *reciprocal* process, just as language is. So that other people treat me as human, I too must treat them as human. If I see them all as objects or as animals, I myself will be no more than an object or an animal. Hence, giving yourself a good life cannot in the end be very different from granting a good life. Please, think about that.

Now, to conclude this chapter in a more relaxed fashion, I propose we go to the movies. If you like, we can see *Citizen Kane*, a wonderful film, directed by and starring Orson Welles. I'll recap it briefly: Kane is a multimillionaire, somewhat unscrupulous, who has accumulated in his palace, Xanadu, a vast collection of most elegant and expensive things. He has everything, no question, and he uses everyone around him for his own ends, simply as instruments of his own ambition. At the end of his life, he paces alone through the great rooms in his mansion, filled with mirrors that reflect back, over and over, his solitary image, all that he has for company. Finally, he dies, muttering a single word: "Rosebud." A reporter tries to decipher the meaning of this last utterance, but without success. Rosebud is the name written on a sled Kane had played with as a child, when he was still surrounded by affection, an affection he returned to those around him. All his wealth, all his power over others, had not been able to bring him anything better than that childhood memory. That sled, recalling a time of gentle human relationships, represented in truth what Kane longed for, the *good life* that he had sacrificed in order to accumulate the thousands of material things that were in reality worthless to him. And even so, the majority of people envied him. Come on, let's go to the movies. We'll continue tomorrow.

Selections for Further Reading

When the boys grew up, Esau was a skillful hunter, a man of the field, while Jacob was a quiet man, dwelling in tents. Isaac loved Esau, because he ate of his game; but Rebekah loved Jacob.

Once when Jacob was boiling pottage, Esau came in from the field, and he was famished. And Esau said to Jacob, "Let me eat some of that red pottage, for I am famished!" Jacob said, "First sell me your birthright." Esau said, "I am about to die; of what use is a birthright to me?" Jacob said, "Swear to me first." So he swore to him, and sold his birthright to Jacob. Then Jacob gave Esau bread and pottage of lentils, and he ate and drank,

and rose and went his way. Thus Esau despised
his birthright.

—Genesis 25:27–34

Perhaps man is evil because throughout his life he
is awaiting death; and so he dies a thousand times
in the death of others and of things.

But then every animal aware of the imminent
danger of death goes mad. Mad-fearful, mad-
crafty, mad-wicked, mad-outlaw, mad-servant and
mad-fulminator, mad-hater, mad-troublemaker,
mad-murderer.

—TONY DUVERT, *A Malevolent Alphabet*

A free man thinks of nothing less than of death,
and his wisdom is a meditation on life, not on
death.

—SPINOZA, *Ethics* II-261

Free is the man that wills without caprice. He
believes in the actual, which is to say: he believes

in the real association of the real duality, I and Thou. He believes in destiny and also that it needs him. It does not lead him, it waits for him. He must proceed toward it without knowing where it waits for him. He must go forth with his whole being: that he knows. It will not turn out the way his resolve intended it; but what wants to come will come only if he resolves to do that which he can will.

—MARTIN BUBER, *I and Thou*

Respect for one's own integrity and uniqueness, love for and understanding of one's own self, cannot be separated from respect for and love and understanding of another individual. The love for my own self is inseparably connected with the love for any other self.

—ERICH FROMM, *Man for Himself: An Inquiry into the Psychology of Ethics*

Wake Up, Baby!

A BRIEF RECAPITULATION: Esau the hunter, reminding himself that life is short, follows the counsels of his stomach and renounces his birthright for a plateful of lentil stew (Jacob was at least generous with the food and allowed him second and third helpings). Citizen Kane devoted many years to selling all his people so that he could buy all his things; and at the end of his life he realizes that if he could he would trade in his palace full of expensive possessions for the one humble object —an old sled—that reminded him of a certain person, namely, himself before he gave himself up to buying and selling, when he preferred

loving and being loved to possessing and domi-
nating.

Both Esau and Kane thought they were doing
what they wanted, but neither one, it would seem,
managed to give himself a good life. If they had
been asked what they really wanted, however, they
would have replied, just as would you or I, "I
want to give myself a good life." So, while what
we all want is clear enough, just what constitutes
this "good life" is not so clear. Wanting a good
life is not just a simple wish, as when we wish for
lentils, pictures, household gadgets, or money.
All these wishes are *simple* ones—they fix on one
simple aspect of our reality, but they have no
overall perspective. There is nothing wrong in
wanting lentil stew when we feel hungry, obviously; but there are many other things in the
world, other connections, obligations from the
past, hopes for the future, many more that you
can think of. Man does not live by lentils alone.
For the sake of his lentil stew, Esau sacrificed too

many important elements in his life; he simplified things much more than he should have. He acted, as I have said, under the weight of imminent death. Death is a great simplifier: When you are about to die, very few things matter beyond the medicine that can save you, the air with which you fill your lungs one more time. Living, on the other hand, is always a complex business, full of complications. If you reject complexity and pursue the great simplification, you don't think of wanting to live longer and better, you want to die, once and for all. And we have said that what we want is a good life, not a quick death. Hence, Esau is not much use to us as a model.

Kane, too, oversimplified the matter in his own way. As distinct from Esau, he was not a spendthrift but an ambitious accumulator. What he wanted was to be able to manipulate men and money in order to acquire many beautiful and useful things. Now, I have nothing against trying to make money, nor against craving beautiful and useful things. I don't trust those people who say money doesn't interest them and who claim not to need anything. Perhaps I am made of inferior clay, but I find nothing appealing in being penniless, and if burglars were to clean out my house and remove all my books (there not being much else for them to take, I fear), I would feel like a victim. The urge to acquire more and more money or things, however, seems to me unhealthy. In truth, the things that we own may retaliate by owning us; our possessions can possess us. Let me explain. A Buddhist sage once said to his disciple just what I am saying to you, and the young man looked at him with the same odd expression that you have on your face while reading this ("This man is crazy!"). The master then asked his pupil, "Of all the things in this room, which do you like best?" The sharp-eyed pupil pointed to a magnificent bowl of gold and ivory. "Very well, pick it up," said the master, and the young man, not needing to be told twice, grasped the precious object in his right hand. "Now don't let go of it," said the master, with some irony; and he added, "Isn't there anything else that you fancy?" There was a bag full of money on the table, which the pupil admitted he was not averse to wanting. "Go on then, take it!" said the master, and the young man grasped it eagerly with his left hand. "And now, what do I do?" he asked his master somewhat nervously. "Now, scratch yourself!" the old man replied. Of course, he could not. Look what happens when he needs to scratch an itch on some part of his body —or his spirit! With his hands full, he cannot scratch or do other things when he needs to. What we have in our grip has us in its grasp—we have to be careful not to exceed ourselves. That is more or less what happened to Kane: His hands and his spirit were so busy with possessions that when he felt an itch he could not scratch.

Life is more complicated than Kane imagined; hands are not just for grasping but also for

scratching oneself or for caressing. But his fundamental mistake was something else, if I am not
mistaken. Obsessed with accumulating money
and things, he treated people as if they too were
things. He thought that that was what was meant
by having power over them. A serious simplification—that is precisely what makes life so complex, the fact that people are not things. At first,
Kane saw no particular difference—he bought
and sold things, and he bought and sold people.
You make use of things as long as they are useful,
and later, you dispose of them. Kane did the very
same with the people around him. He behaved in
that way toward lovers, friends, employees, political rivals, every living thing. Of course, he caused
a great deal of pain in others, but the worst from
his point of view (the point of view of someone
who we must suppose wanted to give himself a
good life) is that he did serious damage to himself.
I will try to enlarge on that for you, for it seems to
me of the greatest importance.

Be clear about this: From things, even the best things, can come only *things*. Nothing can give more than it has, nor can it give more than it is, true? Lentils are useful for relieving hunger, but they will not help you to learn French; money helps in almost every case, but it cannot buy true friendship—it can buy servants, hangers-on, spongers, prostitutes, no more. A television set can lend a part to another television set, but it can't give it a kiss. If we were simply things, what we get from things would be enough for us. But that's where the complications I spoke of crop up: *Since we are not just things, we need "things" that things don't have.* When we treat other people like things, as Kane did, what we get back from them are just things: When we squeeze them, they produce money; they work for us much as machines do; they come, they go, they rub against us, or they smile when we press the appropriate button. But they will never bring to us those subtler rewards that only people can give. We will never get from them friendship or respect, let alone love. No thing (nor animal, since the difference between its condition and ours is too great) can give us friendship, respect, love, or that essential *complicity* that can arise only between equals, that we as people can receive only from other people whom we treat in the same way. The question of treatment is important, for, as we have already said, human beings humanize one another. By treating other people as people, not as things (that is, by taking note of what they want and what they need, and not just what we can get from them), we make it possible for them to give back to us what only people can give to one another.

This small detail escaped Kane, and suddenly, too late, he realized that he had everything except what only other people could give him: sincere respect, or spontaneous affection, or intelligent companionship. Since to Kane nothing ever seemed as important as money, so to other people nothing about Kane seemed important except his money. Besides, the great man knew that it was his own fault. Sometimes you can treat others as people and get back nothing more than blows, betrayals, or abuse. So be it. But you retain the respect of at least *one* person, namely, yourself. In not treating other people as things, we keep the right not to be things to others. We try to make possible a world of people, a human world—a world in which people treat others as they treat themselves, the only one in which we can truly live well. I imagine that the despair Kane felt at the end of his life arose not simply from his having lost the tenderness and human closeness he had had as a child, but from having persisted in ignoring them, and having dedicated his whole life to riding roughshod over them. It is not just that he did not have those human connections, it is that he realized that he did not *deserve* them.

But a great many people certainly admired Kane the multimillionaire, you will say. No doubt many thought, "That man certainly knows how to live!" Kane accumulated everything that he *had heard tell* makes a person happy: money, power, influence, obedience. He found out in the end that, whatever people said, he did not have what was essential: real affection, real respect, the real love of people who were free, whom he could treat as people and not as things. Perhaps Kane was a bit out of the ordinary—protagonists in movies usually are. Many people might have been perfectly satisfied to live in such a palace in such luxury; and the majority, you will insist cynically, would never have given a thought to the sled, Rosebud. Perhaps Kane was somewhat touched in the head—imagine feeling wretched with all the things he had! Now, forget about other people, and think about yourself. This good life that you are after, is it like Kane's? Would you be satisfied with Esau's plate of lentil stew?

Don't answer in a hurry. What ethics looks for is to discover just what makes for a good life *in depth*, beyond what people tell you, beyond what we see in television commercials, that fortunate life we would like to get ahold of. At this level we know that no good life can dispense with things (we need lentils, which contain iron), but even less can we do without people. We have to deal with things as things, and treat people as people. In that way, things will be helpful to us in many ways, and people in one fundamental way, which things cannot provide, namely, that of being *human*. Perhaps being human is not important, since, like it or not, we *are* human, irremediably so. But we can be either thing-human or human-human, the first dedicated simply to acquiring things from life—all kinds of things, the more the better—the second devoted to the *enjoyment* of human life among other people.

I realize that at first many people would not think what I am saying very important. Are they trustworthy? Are they cleverer, or are they simply less concerned with their own lives? It's possible to be brilliant in business or politics, and a complete fool in more serious matters like living well. I pass on to you a word which I think is crucial here: *attention*. I don't mean attention like that of an owl, which does not speak but fixes its gaze; by attention, I mean a readiness to think about what one does, to try to be as clear as possible about the "good life" we want to live. No comfortable but dangerous simplifications, but instead the attempt to understand this business of living life *humanly*, in all its complexity.

I believe that the first and most indispensable ethical condition is that of being determined to live, not just haphazardly, but as though it matters, even although sooner or later we are all going to die. When people speak of "morality," they are usually referring to rules and habits that are generally respected, at least superficially, often without anyone's being very sure why. But perhaps the real secret lies not in submitting to a moral code or going against established thinking (which is also an upside-down way of submitting), but in trying to *understand*—to understand why some kinds of behavior suit us and others don't, to understand what it is that makes life "good" for us humans. Above all, in not being satisfied by simply *being thought good*, seeming good to other people, gaining their *approval*. It will of course be essential not just to have the attention of an owl or the obedience of a robot, but also to speak with other people, to listen to them, to argue and discuss. But as for making decisions, each person must do that for himself: Nobody else can exercise your freedom for you.

For now, I leave you with two questions to think about, to mull over. The first is this: What we call *bad*, why is it bad? The other is much more appealing: What does it mean to treat people as people? If you are patient with me, we will try to answer these questions in the next two chapters.

Selections for
Further Reading

The fact that he is a sociable being is man's weakness—it is our common weakness that inclines us toward humanity in general. If we were not part of it, we would owe it nothing. Every attachment is a sign of our insufficiency: If each one of us had no need of others, we would not think of having anything to do with them. So from that very deficiency is born our fragile fortune. A truly happy being is a solitary being. Only God enjoys absolute happiness, but who among us aspires to the same thing? If someone among us, imperfect as we are, were self-sufficient, in what would he take his pleasure, except in us? He would be alone, he would be miserable. I cannot conceive that someone who needs nothing could love anything; and I cannot imagine that anyone who does not love could be happy.

—JEAN-JACQUES ROUSSEAU, *Emile*

And as for those pretenders whose busy poverty has usurped the name of wealth, they "possess" their riches in the same way that we might be said to possess a fever, namely, it possesses us.

—SENECA, *Letters to Lucilius*

Since virtue is nothing but acting from the laws of one's own nature, and no one strives to preserve his being except from the laws of his own nature, it follows that the foundation of virtue is this very striving to preserve one's own being, and that happiness consists in man's being able to preserve his being. . . . To Man, there is nothing more useful than man. Man, I say, can wish for nothing more helpful to the preservation of his being than that all should so agree in all things that the Minds and Bodies of all would compose, as it were, one Mind and one Body; that all should strive together, as far as they can, to preserve their being; and that all, together, should seek for themselves the common advantage of all.

From this it follows that men who are governed by reason—i.e., men who, from the guidance of reason, seek their own advantage—want nothing for themselves that they do not desire for other men. Hence, they are just, honest, and honorable.

—SPINOZA, *Ethics* II-222

Here Comes
Jiminy Cricket

D O YOU KNOW the only *obligation* we have in this life? Not to be imbeciles. There's a lot more to the word "imbecile" than meets the eye, believe me. It comes from the Latin *baculus*, which means "walking stick," so an imbecile is someone who needs a walking stick. Now, don't turn on the lame or the old, for the stick here is not the one that old people or accident victims use to support themselves or to take a few steps. An imbecile can be as nimble as anyone, springing about like an Olympic gazelle; that's not what it's about. An imbecile's lameness is not in his legs, it's in his spirit. His being is enfeebled and crip-

pled, although his body may be turning somer-
saults.

There are various types of imbecile:

■ One who thinks that he lacks nothing,
who says that he doesn't care, who lives in
an everlasting yawn or a permanent siesta,
even though his eyes are open and he
doesn't snore.

■ One who wants everything, the first
thing that comes to mind, and its opposite at
the same time: to go for a walk and stay in
his chair, to dance and to remain seated, to
chew garlic and kiss divinely, all at the same
time.

■ One who has no idea what he wants and
doesn't bother to find out. He either falls in
completely with the ways of his neighbors or
takes against them—everything he does reflects the majority opinion of those around

him. He is an unthinking conformist or a rebel without a cause.

■ One who knows that he wants, knows what he wants, and knows more or less why he wants it; but his wanting is too weak, timid, and spineless. He always ends up doing what he doesn't want and leaving what he wants for the next day, in case things prove more propitious.

■ One who wants with a wilful and reckless ferocity, but who has deceived himself about what is real. He wanders far from the track, and ends up confusing the good life with the very thing that is going to destroy him.

All these kinds of imbecile need a walking stick, that is, they need to lean on outside things, things quite alien to freedom and clear thinking. I am sorry to say that imbeciles usually finish up badly, whatever anyone thinks. When I say they "finish up badly," I don't mean that they end up in jail or are struck by lightning—that only happens in movies. I mean that they usually are angry at themselves, and never manage to taste the good life that so appeals to us. I am still sorrier to inform you that the symptoms of imbecility turn up in almost all of us; at least, I find them in myself from one day to another. I hope you have better fortune. Conclusion? Watch out! Be on your guard! Imbecility stalks you and does not excuse you!

Please don't confuse this imbecility with the normal use of the word, which refers to idiots, to those who are ignorant, who don't understand trigonometry or cannot master the subjunctive of French verbs. One can be an idiot in mathematics (like me) and not at all in the moral sense, in the sense of the good life. And vice versa: There are those who are wizards in business and perfect cretins in questions of ethics. I'm sure there are

Nobel Prize winners, preeminent in their fields, who trip up and stumble over those questions we are asking. But to avoid imbecility in any form, it is essential to pay attention, and to fortify yourself as much as possible through what you learn. These requirements are the physics and archaeology of ethics. But the business of living well is not the same as knowing two plus two. Knowing your arithmetic is fine, no question, but such knowledge will not save a moral imbecile from calamity.

The opposite of being a moral imbecile is having a *conscience*. But a conscience is not something that you win in the lottery, or that falls on you from the skies. Of course, it must be acknowledged that some people from early childhood are on a better ethical "wavelength" than others, and have an inherent "good taste," morally speaking; this wavelength and good taste can be strengthened and developed in practice, like a good musical ear, or aesthetic good taste. But what about those who are not on such a wavelength and ut-

terly lack such taste in questions of living well?
Well, I'm afraid I see no solution there. You can
come up with all kinds of aesthetic arguments,
invoking the history of art and theories of form
and color, whatever you want, to show that a
Velázquez painting like *Las Meninas* has greater
artistic value than a lithograph of the Ninja Tur-
tles. But if after all your argument some people
say they still prefer the lithograph, I don't know
how to go about correcting their taste. Similarly,
if someone sees nothing wrong in beating a baby
to death with a hammer in order to steal its paci-
fier, I'm afraid that we'd become hoarse long before we convinced him of his error.

I do admit that in order to develop a conscience some innate qualities are necessary, just as
they are in order to have an ear for music or an
eye for art. So also are certain social and economic conditions. Someone who has been deprived since the cradle of an essential humanity
will not be as able to grasp what a good life con-

sists of as those who have had better luck. Beyond that, I think the rest depends on both attention and application. But what makes up this conscience that will cure our moral imbecility? It has the following fundamental characteristics:

- knowing that not everything is the same, because we truly wish to live, to live well and *humanly*
- being ready to make sure that what we do is really what we want to do
- continuing to develop good taste in the moral sense, to a point where some things repel us (so that, for example, lying becomes just as offensive as pissing in the soup before it is served)
- giving up looking for excuses to obscure the fact that we are free and hence reasonably responsible for the consequences of our actions.

As you see, in these guidelines I give no other reason for preferring having a conscience over moral imbecility than that of your own advantage. What is this *bad* we talk about? It is anything that prevents us from living the good life we are after. Does that mean then that we should avoid the bad through a kind of egoism? Just that. As it is commonly used, the word "egoism" has a dubious reputation: An egoist is someone who thinks only of himself, and has no concern for others, to the point of inconveniencing them without a thought if he will gain some advantage from it. We can say that Kane was an egoist in this sense, as was Caligula, that Roman emperor who would commit any crime to satisfy his merest whim.

But are these monstrous characters we call egoists really egoists? Who is the real egoist? Who manages to be an egoist without being a moral imbecile? Surely *he who wants the best for himself,* what we call the good life. Did Kane have a good life? It doesn't seem so, as Orson Welles tells it.

He made a practice of treating people as though they were objects and so was deprived of the more desirable of human rewards: sincere and loving relationships, immeasurable friendships. And Caligula? Look what a life he gave himself! The only real feelings he stirred up in others were fear and hatred. You have to be a true moral imbecile to suppose that it is better to live in the company of fear and cruelty than among love and well-wishing. In the end, it was his own guards who took on the task of dispatching him. Some egoist, if he hoped to have a good life founded on all his wrongdoing! If he had really thought of himself —that's to say, if he had had a conscience—he would have realized that what we humans need to live well is something only other people can give us if we are worthy of it, something it is impossible to steal by force or deceit. When it is bought or stolen, that something—respect, friendship, love—loses all its savor and most likely turns to poison. Egoists like Kane and Caligula are like those contestants in *One Two Three* or *The Price Is Right*, who are after the big prize but go wrong, choosing the hand with nothing in it.

The only ones who truly deserve to be called egoists are those who really know what suits them and what they need to live well, and who push themselves to attain these things. A person whose head is full of things that torture him (hatred, criminal impulses, lentils paid for in tears) would like deep down to be an egoist but *doesn't know how.* He belongs to the imbecile family, and would have to adjust his conscience a bit before he could like himself better. For this poor creature (poor millionaire, poor emperor; it makes no difference) believes that he is in tune with himself but gives so little attention to what would really suit him that he ends up acting as his own worst enemy. Such is the case with Richard III, the iniquitous villain of Shakespeare's tragedy. On his way to becoming king, the Duke of Gloucester (who will be crowned as Richard III) murders all members of the male line, children among them, who come between him and the throne. Gloucester is perceptive and quick-witted but deformed, which causes a deep anguish in him. He imagines that real power will in some way compensate for his hunched back and his withered leg, and gain him the respect that his physical appearance cannot command. Gloucester wishes to be loved; he feels cast out because of his deformity, and thinks that respect and affection can be wrung from others. He wins the throne but the affection of no one; instead he inspires first horror and then hate. The worst is that a man who committed all his crimes out of a desperation within himself now can feel for himself only loathing and horror; he has not only gained no friends but also has lost the only love he could count on, his self-regard. Then the play delivers a terrifying and prophetic diagnosis of his condition:

I'll join with black despair against my soul,
And to myself become an enemy.

(Richard III, II.ii.36)

Why did Richard become his own enemy?
Didn't he get what he wanted, the throne? Yes,
but at the cost of losing whatever chance he had
of being loved and respected by the rest of humanity. A crown does not automatically attract
love or real respect; it can only command flattery,
fear, and servility, especially when, as in Richard's
case, it was gained nefariously. Instead of com-
pensating for his physical deformity, his lust
for power deforms his mind. Neither his hump
nor his lame leg are to blame—these unfortunate irregularities are not in themselves any
cause for shame. The ones who ought to have
been ashamed were those who mocked him, who
looked down on him as a cripple. From the outside people saw him as deformed, but from inside
he thought of himself as intelligent, generous,

worthy of affectionate regard. Had he truly valued himself, he would have tried in all he did to externalize his just, well-meaning interior self. But the contrary occurred: His many crimes turned him into a monster much more repellent than his deformities made him, as he saw when he looked deeply inside himself, where there are no witnesses. Why? Because he was responsible for his moral hump and limp, while those physical infirmities were accidents of nature. His crown, stained by betrayal and blood, does not win him love. Quite the reverse: Now he knows himself to be unworthy of love, for he is unable to love himself. Can we call someone who does such harm to himself an egoist?

In the previous paragraph, I have used some heavy words, as you may have noticed, words like "blame" and "responsible." They are the kind of words mostly used in talking about conscience, aren't they—used by Jiminy Cricket and the rest. I only have to mention the heaviest word of all:

"remorse." What embittered Richard and kept him from enjoying throne and power was the remorse he suffered in his conscience. Now, tell me, where does remorse spring from? In certain cases, remorse reflects the inner fear that we feel of the dire punishment that our wrongdoings probably well deserve, either in this world or the next. But let's suppose that Richard has no fear of being brought to justice, and does not believe in any god who will condemn him to eternal fire for his atrocities. Even so, he suffers a constant remorse. A person can suffer remorse over things he has done *even though he may be reasonably sure that nobody and nothing will take revenge on him.* The fact is that whenever we do harm and then realize what we have done, we know that we are already being punished, and that to a greater or lesser degree we have harmed ourselves of our own free will. There is no greater punishment than realizing that because of what we are doing we are making more inaccessible the very existence we long for.

But where does remorse come from? It seems clear to me that it comes from our *freedom*. If we were not free, we would be able to feel neither guilt nor pride about anything, and we would not feel remorse. Hence, when we know we have done something outrageous, we try to convince ourselves that we had no choice but to act as we did: "I was carrying out the orders of my superiors"; "As far as I could see, everybody else was doing the same"; "I lost my head"; "It was stronger than I am"; "I didn't realize what I was doing." Small children make similar excuses. When a jar of marmalade they have been trying to reach on a high shelf falls and breaks, they will claim tearfully, "It wasn't me!" They say that precisely because *they know that they did it*. If they had not, they wouldn't bother to say anything, and might even laugh about it. But if they have made an eye-catching drawing, they will tell you over and over, "I did it on my own, nobody helped me!" We who are older act the same way: We always choose to be free to claim for ourselves any merit in what we do, but when what we do does not turn out well, we prefer to call ourselves victims of circumstance.

Let's be rid once and for all of that irritating pedant Jiminy Cricket; to me he has always been a truly uncongenial creature, like that other detestable insect, the ant in the fable who leaves the feeble-minded grasshopper outside all winter without food or shelter, to teach it a lesson— monstrous behavior! It's all a matter of taking freedom very seriously or, in other words, being *responsible*. Freedom is a serious matter since it has unquestionable effects that, once set in motion, cannot be erased or recalled on whim. I am free to eat or not eat this pastry in front of me; but once I have eaten it, I am not free to have it in front of me. Another example, from Aristotle, the

Greek sage of the boat and the storm: If I have a stone in my hand, I am free to throw it or hold on to it; but if I throw it some distance, I cannot order it to return to my hand. And if I kill someone with it? The serious thing about freedom is that every free choice I make, every time I choose something and pursue it, I am narrowing my own possibilities. There's no point in trying to find out whether something has succeeded or failed before accepting the responsibility for it. Perhaps you will manage to deceive outsiders, as the child who protests "It wasn't me!" tries to do, but you cannot deceive yourself. Ask Richard. Ask Pinocchio.

So, what we call remorse is nothing more than the dissatisfaction we feel with ourselves when we have used our freedom badly, when we have acted contradictorily to what we really want as human beings. Accepting responsibility is being truly free, for better or for worse; it is facing up to the consequences of what we have done, correcting the bad where it can be corrected, and making the most of what is good. As distinct from the unfortunate child, a responsible person is ready to *answer* for his actions, to say, "Yes, it was me!" If you think of it, the world around us is full of pretexts for shedding the weight of responsibility. It seems that anything bad that happens is blamed on circumstances, or the society we live in, or the capitalist system, or character ("It's just the way I am!"), or a bad education, or having been spoiled, or television commercials, or all the temptations on display everywhere, pernicious and irresistible. I have just used a word central to all these excuses: "irresistible." All those who want to shed responsibility believe in the irresistible nature of whatever enslaves them, be it propaganda, drugs, appetites, bribes, threats, ways of being, whatever crops up. As soon as the Irresistible manifests itself, *zap!*—people cast aside their freedom and become puppets moved by something outside of them, unworthy of them. Authoritarian personalities believe firmly in the Irresistible, and consider it essential to get rid of everything that could prove addictive and enslaving. Once the police have stamped out all temptation, there will be no more crime—and no more freedom either, of course, no gain without pain. Think of the huge relief in knowing that if any loose temptation comes along, the responsibility for what happens lies with those who failed to wipe it out in time, not with those who succumb to it.

What if I tell you that this Irresistible is nothing more than a superstition conjured up by those who are afraid of their own freedom? That all the theories and institutions that offer to relieve us of our responsibilities want not our well-being but our enslavement to them? That anyone who waits until the world is "as it should be" before acting "as he should" is an idiot? That for all the restrictions they put on us, for all the police who eye us constantly, we can still do harm, harm to ourselves, if we want to? I am telling you these things with all the conviction I can summon.

The great Argentine poet and storyteller Jorge Luis Borges reflects at the beginning of one of his stories on an ancestor of his: "For him, as for all men, the times were bad to live in." Nobody has ever lived in utterly peaceful times, when being alive and having a good life were easy. There have always been violence, rape, cowardice, imbecility, moral or otherwise, lies taken for truths because they are more pleasing to the ear. A good life does not come as a gift—nobody gets what suits him without both nerve and energy. The only thing I can guarantee you is that our world has never been a utopia, but that each one of us must take for himself the decision to live a good life as he sees it, without waiting for favorable conditions, for the rest of the world to urge him on.

The essence of responsibility, if you are interested, is not just having the grace and the decency to accept one's own blunders without looking for excuses left and right. A responsible person is well aware of how *real* his freedom is. I use the word "real" in its senses of "genuine" and "true," but also in the sense of "royal": A king must make decisions without anyone above him to give orders. Being responsible is knowing that each act of mine is bringing me into being, defining me, *inventing* me. In choosing what I choose I *transform* myself, little by little. All my decisions leave their mark in me before they leave any in the world around me. And certainly, once I have used my freedom to face up to myself, I can't complain or take fright at the person who looks at me from the mirror. If I move toward a good life it will be more difficult for me to live badly (though unfortunately the reverse is also true). The ideal is to acquire the vice of living well! When a hero in a Western gets the chance to shoot the outlaw in the back and says, "But I just *can't*!" we all know what he means. He could certainly fire, pull the trigger; it's just that he doesn't do such things. The "good" heroes and heroines of history stand for something. They want to remain faithful to the kind of person they have chosen to be, the person they freely put together for themselves at a previous stage.

Forgive me for letting this chapter run on—I got carried away, and besides I have so many things to tell you! We'll leave it here and gather our strength, for next I want to talk about treating people as people, and being well disposed toward them.

Selections for Further Reading

O coward conscience, how dost thou afflict me?
The lights burn blue. It is now dead midnight.
Cold fearful drops stand on my trembling flesh.

What do I fear? Myself? There's none else by.
Richard loves Richard; that is, I am I.
Is there a murderer here? No. Yes, I am.
Then fly! What, from myself? Great reason.
  Why?
Lest I revenge. Myself upon myself?
Alack, I love myself. Wherefore? For any good
That I myself have done unto myself?
O no, alas, I rather hate myself
For hateful deeds committed by myself.
I am a villain. Yet I lie: I am not.
Fool, of thyself speak well.—Fool, do not
  flatter.
My conscience hath a thousand several tongues,
And every tongue brings in a several tale,
And every tale condemns me for a villain.
Perjury, perjury, in the high'st degree!
Murder, stern murder, in the dir'st degree!
All several sins, all used in each degree,
Throng to the bar, crying all, "Guilty, guilty!"
I shall despair. There is no creature loves me,

And if I die no soul will pity me.
Nay, wherefore should they?—Since that I
  myself
Find in myself no pity to myself.
      —SHAKESPEARE, *Richard III* (V.v.133–157)

*"Do not do to others what you would not have them
do to you"* is one of the most fundamental principles of ethics. But it is equally justifiable to state:
Whatever you do to others, you also do to yourself.
      —ERICH FROMM, *Man for Himself: An Inquiry
into the Psychology of Ethics*

One never helps another without thereby helping
himself. When I say this I'm not talking about
wanting to assist someone when you yourself have
been assisted, or to protect someone because you
have been protected, or that a good example cir-
cles back to the benefit of the doer (just as mal-
efactors are haunted by their past deeds, having
squandered our sympathy when it is their turn to

suffer after their own fashion at the hands of others); instead, I'm saying that a virtuous act is its own reward. For it is not undertaken for profit: the real compensation of a right action is inherent in having performed it.

—SENECA, *Letters to Lucilius*

Put Yourself
in His Place

ROBINSON CRUSOE walks on one of the beaches of the island on which he has been cast up from his shipwreck by an unforeseen storm. His parrot perches on his shoulder, and he is protected from the sun by a parasol fashioned from palm leaves, which makes him justifiably proud of his own handiwork. He is thinking that under the circumstances he has not done badly— he now has a shelter to protect him from weather and wild animals, he can procure both food and drink, he has clothes he has fashioned from natural materials, he has tamed a flock of goats to his uses. To allow himself to live a good life as a castaway, he has managed to make ingenious use of what the island has. He continues his walk, so content in himself that for a moment he thinks that really he wants for nothing. All of a sudden, he comes to a startled stop. There in the white sand is a mark that will turn his equable existence upside down; it is the print of a human foot.

Whose? Friend or enemy? An enemy who can be made into a friend? Man or woman? How will he approach him—or her? How will he *treat* him? Since he landed on the island, Robinson has made a habit of asking himself questions and solving his problems in the simplest and most ingenious way: What will I eat? Where will I take shelter? How will I protect myself from the sun? But now, the situation is different—it's not just a matter of dealing with the natural world, with hunger or rain or wild animals, but with another human being, another Robinson, if you like, or other Robinsons, male or female. In the face of the elements and the animals, Robinson could live with just a single concern: his need to survive. Dealing with the natural world is a straightforward matter, but dealing with human beings is not so simple a business. Survival still comes first, of course, but not just raw survival. If Robinson through his solitude and his misfortune has turned into an animal like those around him, he will not be perturbed over whether the author of the footprint is an enemy to be killed or a prey to be devoured. But if he still wishes to go on being human, the footprint will not represent enemy or prey but rather a rival or a possible companion; in any case, a fellow human.

While he is alone, Robinson tackles all kinds of problems—technical, mechanical, hygienic, and scientific—anything that is pertinent to *surviving* in hostile and unknown surroundings. But when he comes across Friday's footprint in the sand, he is now faced with *ethical* questions. Now it's not just a question of surviving, like an animal or an artichoke; now he has to begin to live humanly, with others or against them, but at least among them. What makes life *human* is what goes on in human company: speaking with others, agreeing with them or lying to them, being respected or being betrayed, loving, making plans, remembering the past, challenging, organizing common pursuits, playing, exchanging symbols. Ethics takes no interest in how to eat better, how better to protect oneself from the cold, or how to ford a river without drowning, matters of unquestionable importance in certain circumstances. The focus of ethics, its specialty, if you like, is how to live a human life among human beings, and live it well. If we don't know enough about how to confront natural dangers in order to survive, we lose our lives, which is a major disaster; but if we have no idea about ethics, we miss altogether what is human in our lives, a fate that has no appeal whatsoever.

I said earlier that the footprint in the sand informed Robinson of the involving presence of a fellow human being; but, as fellow men, to what extent do Friday and Robinson resemble one another? Robinson is a seventeenth-century man, aware of the considerable advances in scientific knowledge, educated in the Christian religion, a reader of Homer and of the printed book; Friday is a savage, a cannibal from the South Seas, his only language and culture coming from the oral tradition of his tribe, a believer in many gods, utterly ignorant of the existence of great cities like London and Amsterdam. Everything about the two men is different: color of skin, tastes in food, diversions—I would guess that not even their dreams have anything in common. In spite of so many differences, however, there is in both of them something fundamentally similar, an essential fellowship that Robinson cannot feel for any animal or tree or spring on the island. First of all, both of them can *speak,* albeit in different languages. Their world is made of symbols and the relations between symbols, not just of things with no name. Each of them is quite capable of appraising how people behave, aware that some acts are "good," others "bad." At first, their notions of good and bad are very far apart, since their actual values come from very different cultures. Take for a start the case of cannibalism, something quite allowable and acceptable to Friday, but to Robinson as horrible a practice as he could think of, as it probably is to you. In spite of that, the two concur in assuming that there are standards that help indicate what is acceptable and what is repulsive. Although they begin from very distinct positions, they are able to converse, and to understand what they are discussing, which is a good deal more than you can do with a shark or an avalanche of rocks, no?

That's all very well, you say, but no matter how alike people are, they have difficulty deciding in advance the best way of behaving toward each other. If the footprint in the sand had been that of a member of a cannibal tribe that consumed its victims instantly, Robinson's attitude would not have been the same as it would be, say, toward the cabin boy from the boat returned to rescue him. It is precisely because other men are so like me that they can be more dangerous to me than wild beasts or an earthquake. There is no enemy more dangerous than an intelligent one, who can devise intricate plans, lay traps, and catch me out in a thousand different ways. Perhaps it would be better to seize the initiative and set on them first through violence and ambush, treating them as if they were already the enemies they could become. This attitude is not, however, as wise as it first appears: If I appear as an enemy to my fellow men, I increase the risk of turning them into my sworn enemies; besides that, I forfeit the chance of winning their friendship, or of keeping it if at first they seem well disposed toward me.

Here's another way of behaving toward our dangerous fellows. Marcus Aurelius was both a Roman emperor and a philosopher, an unusual concurrence inasmuch as those who govern are not normally interested in questions that are not primarily practical. He made a practice of taking notes, turning his ideas into conversations with himself, in the course of which he would give himself advice or scold himself. He often made entries like the following: "When you first rise in the morning, reflect that in the course of the day you may very well meet a liar, or a thief, or an adulterer, or a murderer. Remember that you must treat them as men, for they are as human as you are and hence as necessary to you as the lower jaw is to the upper." For Marcus Aurelius, the most important thing about other people is not whether their behavior meets with our approval; it is much more that they, as human beings, are necessary to us, and we must never lose sight of that in our dealings with others. However much harm they have done, their humanity is similar to my humanity, and sustains it. Without others, I could perhaps live, but I could not live humanly. Although I have a false tooth and two or three cavities, it is always best at mealtime to be able to rely on a lower jaw to help the upper.

It is the common possession of an intelligence, of the ability to calculate and project, of passions and fears, that makes others dangerous when they wish to be, but also supremely *useful.* When a true sympathy occurs between human beings, when someone else pleases and impresses, there is nothing better in the world. Do you know anything better than the feeling of being loved? When someone goes after money, or power, or prestige, doesn't he want that wealth in order to acquire a portion of that love which those who are loved receive gratis? And only another human being is capable of that love, someone who has a being similar to ours, who loves us inasmuch as we are human, and even in spite of it. No favorite animal, however affectionate it may be, is able to give as much as another human being, even someone not particularly likable.

It is true, however, that I approach other people with a certain wariness, a wariness that does not come from distrust or suspicion but is more like the care I take in handling something fragile, the most delicate of things. Since bonds of respect and friendship with others are to me the most valuable things there are, I take great care of them, and my main concern is to protect and even cherish them, even when it seems I should be saving my own skin.

Marcus Aurelius—emperor, philosopher, and certainly no fool—knew very well, as do you, that there are people who rob, lie, and kill. He naturally did not suppose that his concern for others included condoning their conduct. But he made two points that seem most important to me:

ONE. Anyone who robs, deceives, betrays, violates, kills, or somehow abuses others does not cease to be human. Language misleads us: When we pin on someone a derogatory label like "thief," "liar," or "criminal," it causes us to forget

that individuals who have behaved unacceptably
are human beings, and remain human beings.
Someone who has grown hateful in our eyes can,
since he is a human being, change essentially into
someone who will appeal to us.

TWO. One of our main human characteristics is
our ability to *imitate*. Most of our behavior and
our tastes we copy from others. We are avid to
learn, and we never stop acquiring the knowledge
arrived at by others in past times and far places.
All that we call "civilization" or "culture" is com-
posed of a modicum of invention and a great deal
of imitation. If we were not such imitators, each
man would have to begin all over again from zero.
Hence, the *example* we show to our fellows is of
supreme importance, since in most cases, we will
almost certainly be treated by others as they themselves are treated. If we are generally antagonistic
in our behavior, even obliquely, it is unlikely we
will get back anything more than antagonism. I
know also that however good an example anyone

sets, there are always too many bad examples for
other people to follow. Why take the trouble, why
give up the easy gains that less scrupulous people
regularly go after? Marcus Aurelius has an obser-
vation for you: "Does it seem wise to add to the
already vast number of bad people from whom
very little can be expected that is positive? Does it
seem wise to discourage the minority of right-
thinking people who can help you in so many
ways to live a good life? Does it not make more
sense to plant what you hope to harvest instead of
its opposite, even when you know that weeds may
destroy your harvest? Will you choose to behave
in arbitrary and unpredictable ways, instead of
holding up and demonstrating the advantages of
good sense?"

Let's look a little more closely at the behavior
of those whom we call bad people, those who treat
their fellow creatures as enemies instead of culti-
vating their friendship. You must remember the
movie *Frankenstein*, with that lovable monster of

monsters Boris Karloff. We tried to watch it together on television when you were quite small, and I had to switch it off because you said to me with disarming frankness, "It's getting *too* scary for me." Well, in the novel by Mary Shelley on which the movie is based, the monster put together from pieces of dead bodies confesses to his now regretful inventor: "I am wicked because I am wretched." I believe that the great majority of supposedly bad people in the world could in all sincerity say the same thing. If they are hostile and disrespectful to others, it is because they feel fearful and isolated, because they lack the essential things that most other people have, or because they suffer the worst disgrace, that of being treated by the majority with neither love nor respect, as happened to Dr. Frankenstein's poor creature, who was befriended only by a blind man and a young girl. I know of no one who is perfectly happy being bad, or who would kill his neighbor from pure joy. There are plenty of people all the same who for their peace of mind need to shut out the sufferings of those around them, and in some sense they are accomplices. Ignorance, however satisfied it may feel, is another form of misfortune.

Now, if it is true that the happier we are the less likely we are to turn bad, would it not be sensible to try as much as possible to foster the well-being of others instead of treating them as disgraced, and so turning them to the bad? A person who brings about the misfortune of someone else, and who does nothing to relieve it, is asking for it, and has no right to complain about the number of bad people in the world. In the short run, treating others as enemies or as victims may seem advantageous. The world is full of con men and shady characters who pride themselves on their skills at taking advantage of the goodwill of others, and even of their misfortunes. They don't seem to me at all as sharp as they claim to be. The greatest advantage we can draw from our fellows is not the acquisition of more things or power over more people to treat as things or instruments; it is *the shared understanding and affection of other free spirits,* which means also the expansion and reinforcement of our own humanity. "So what is that good for, how will it serve you?" a cynic will ask you, and you will tell him that only servants serve, and that we are talking about human beings who are free. The cynic does not realize that freedom neither serves nor likes to be served; it is looking to infect others. The cynic has a slave mentality, poor fellow, however astute he may think himself.

The cynic sighs and asks tentatively, "If I don't take advantage of others, surely they will take advantage of me?" This is a matter of rats and lions, with a respectful nod to both species. First difference between rats and lions: A rat asks, "What will happen to me?" while a lion asks, "What will I do?" Second difference: The rat wants all others to love him so as to be able to love himself, while the lion loves himself and so is able to love all others. Third difference: A rat will do anything at all to others to prevent them from doing something to him, while a lion believes that any benefit he brings to others benefits himself. To be rat or to be lion—that is the question! To the lion, it's clear enough—clear as twilight, as the poet Antonio Machado might put it—that when we do harm to others the first person harmed is our own self, and that the more courageous we are, the less servile.

Let's try to answer the question we raised some time ago: What does it mean to treat others as human beings? The answer consists simply of trying *to put yourself in the place of the other.* To recognize another as a fellow creature means to be able to understand him from within, to take on momentarily his point of view. This is something we can do only in a playful and uncertain way with a bat or a geranium, but is an essential obligation to others who understand the same symbols as we do. In the end, whenever we speak with someone else we are laying down a common territory in which my "I" can become your "you" and vice versa. If we can't recognize that we have something fundamental in common (the possibility of being for another person what that person is for us), then we cannot exchange anything, not even words. When we can recognize a common humanity with someone, we realize that we belong to each other, that we are both on the same side. This is so even if I am young and the other old, if we are man and woman, white and black, dull-witted and intelligent, healthy and infirm, rich and poor. In the words of an old Roman poet, "I am human, and nothing that is human is alien to me." Being aware of my own humanity means realizing that in spite of all the very real differences between individuals, I am also in some way *inside* the being of all my fellow creatures.

It is not simply a matter of being able to speak with other people. Putting yourself in another's place means a great deal more than starting up symbolic communications with him; it means taking into account his *rights*, and, failing that, it means understanding his reasoning. That is something every man deserves from his fellows, however wretched he may be. He has a right, a human right, to have someone else put himself in his place, to understand what he does and what he feels, even if it means condemning him by the laws that our society has agreed to. Putting yourself in another person's place means *taking the other person seriously*, allowing him as much reality as you claim for yourself. Remember our old friends Kane and Richard? They took themselves with such seriousness and were so mindful of their own ambitions and wishes that other people became not quite real but more like puppets or ghosts. They didn't even try to put themselves in the place of others, or to see their own interests as in any way related to the interests of others. And you know what happened to them.

I am not saying to you that there is anything bad in attending to your own interests or that you should always put them aside for those of your neighbor. Yours of course are every bit as deserving as his. But look at that word "interests." It comes from the Latin *inter esse*, meaning between human beings, and applies to what connects you to other people. When I speak of your own interests as relative, I mean that these interests are not yours in exclusivity, as if you were living alone in a world of ghosts; I am speaking of those matters that put you in touch with other realities quite as real as yours. Hence all the interests you have are relative—dependent on the interests of others, on circumstances, on the laws and customs of the society you live in. All except for one, the only *absolute* interest, namely, the interest in being a human being among other human beings, treating others humanly and being so treated, without which a good life would prove impossible. However much something may interest you, it cannot, if you think about it, be anywhere as interesting to you as is putting yourself in the shoes of someone with whom you are connected. By putting yourself in another's place, you must be able not only to muster all his arguments but also to sense his feelings, his sufferings, his longings, his pleasures. It's a question of feeling sympathy, or compassion, if you prefer, of being able to share in some way a oneness with another, and not leaving him in his solitude of thoughts and desires. It is recognizing that we are made of the same clay, which is at once idea and passion and flesh.

Taking another person seriously, that is, being able to put yourself in his place to a point where he is as real as you are to yourself, doesn't mean that you always think him right in what he demands or in what he does. Nor should you get the notion that you and he are identical, however close you are in some things. The playwright Bernard Shaw used to say, "Don't always do to others what you would like them to do to you—their tastes could be very different from yours." People resemble one another, unquestionably, and it would undoubtedly be a gain if we were all equal in terms of opportunity and before the law, but we are not identical and there is no reason why we should try to be so. Putting yourself in the place of another means trying for a kind of objectivity, trying to see things as another might see them, not imposing yourself on someone else, or taking him over—he has to go on being himself and you have to go on being yourself. Our first human right is the right not to be a photocopy of our neighbors, but to be more or less unique or exceptional. And we have no right to demand of anyone else that they be other than they are, unless of course they are harming someone else.

I just used the term "right" because a large part of the difficult art of putting yourself in the place of another has to do with what has always been called *justice*. Here, however, I am not referring to justice as a public institution (the body of law, judges, lawyers) but to justice as a human virtue, as the insight and interest we must exert to understand what our fellow creatures can expect of us. Laws and judges must try to determine the minimum amount that people can claim from others with whom they have lived, but always the minimum, nothing more. In many cases, however legal our acts, however much we observe the law and avoid fines or imprisonment, our behavior remains fundamentally unjust. Written law is nothing more than an abridgement, a simplification, often imperfect, of what your fellow man can expect from *you*, not from the state or its judiciary. Life is much too subtle and complex, people are too different, situations too varied and often too intimate, for everything to fit into a manual of jurisprudence. Just as no one else can feel your freedom for you, neither can anyone else act justly for you if you haven't realized that being just is a part of living well. To understand completely what another person may want of you, you have to love them a little, even if it is only loving them for their humanity; and that small but most important gesture of love can never be demanded from you by any imposed law. One who lives well must be capable of sympathetic justice, or just compassion.

Another long chapter; but my excuse is that this chapter is the most important one. In these last pages, I have tried to establish the basis of the ethics I speak about. I'd ask you, if you are not too tired, to read it again before you go any further. If you don't, however, I think I will!

Selections for Further Reading

It happened one day about noon, going towards my boat, I was exceedingly surprised with the print of a man's naked foot on the shore, which was very plain to be seen in the sand. I stood like one thunderstruck, or as if I had seen an apparition; I listened, I looked round me, I could hear nothing, nor see anything. . . .

—DANIEL DEFOE, *Robinson Crusoe*

Every true life is an encounter.

—MARTIN BUBER, *I and Thou*

United with his fellow-men by the strongest of all ties, the tie of a common doom, the free man finds that a new vision is with him always, shedding over every daily task the light of love. The life of Man is a long march through the night, surrounded by invisible foes, tortured by weariness and pain, towards a goal that few can hope to reach, and where none may tarry long. One by one, as they march, our comrades vanish from our sight, seized by the silent orders of omnipotent Death. Very brief is the time in which we can help them, in which their happiness or misery is decided. Be it ours to shed sunshine on their path, to lighten their sorrows by the balm of sympathy, to give them the pure joy of a never-tiring affection, to strengthen failing courage, to instil faith in hours of despair.

—BERTRAND RUSSELL, *Mysticism and Logic*

The most hard-faced eulogist of virtue and the grimmest enemy of pleasure, while they invite us to toil and sleepless nights and mortification, still admonish us to relieve the poverty and misfortune of others as best we can. It is especially praise-worthy, they tell us, when we provide for the comfort and welfare of our fellow creatures. Nothing is more humane (and humanity is the virtue most proper to human beings) than to relieve the misery of others, assuage their griefs, and by removing all sadness from their lives, to restore them to enjoyment, that is, pleasure.

—THOMAS MORE, *Utopia*

So Much
Pleasure

S UPPOSE THAT someone tells you that your
friends Dick and Jane have been arrested for
behaving immorally in public. You can be sure
that their "immorality" has not been to drive
through a red light, or tell a huge lie in a public
place, or snatch a handbag in a crowd. More
likely, Dick said something indelicate to a fat
lady, or Jane, after a drink or two, exposed too
much of her extraordinary anatomy. If someone
we would call "respectable" (as if others were
not!) tells you in a grave voice that such and such
a film is "immoral," you can be sure he doesn't
mean that it shows a few murders, or deals with

extortion—you know very well what he is talking about.

When people use the word "moral" and talk about "immorality," eighty percent of the time, if not more, they are talking about sex, so much so that you would think that the word "moral" refers exclusively to what people do with their genitals. Nothing could be more absurd. There is nothing more immoral about sex than there is about eating or going for a walk in the country. Obviously, someone can behave badly in sexual matters (using sex to harm someone else, for example). And of course, since sexual relations can involve a serious attachment and a complexity of delicate feelings, it is natural that our true concern for others should show in such circumstances. There is nothing *bad* about what two people do for their pleasure, harming nobody—truly the bad is in the mind of someone who considers pleasure bad in itself. It's not so much that we *have* a body, as they usually say, but rather that we *are* a body, whose satisfaction and well-being we must provide for if we are to have any kind of good life.

Now, one of the most important functions of sex is procreation, no question—I hardly need to mention it, since you are my son—and it is not to be taken lightly, for with it come important ethical considerations. Think back to what I said before about responsibility being the other half, the twin of freedom. Sex can't simply be limited to procreation. In human beings, the natural impulse toward perpetuating the species has other dimensions biology seems not to have foreseen. Symbols and refinements are added, wonderful inventions arising from that freedom without which we would not be human. It is paradoxical that those who see sex as something bad or disturbing are the ones who with great enthusiasm try to animalize mankind. Only animals use sex for procreation alone, as they use food to fuel themselves, and physical movement to remain healthy. Humans on the other hand have in-

vented eroticism, gastronomy, and athletic compe-
tition. Sex is a mechanism for reproduction to us,
as it is to deer and fish; but it leads human beings
to all kinds of inventions, like lyric poetry and the
institution of marriage (for better or for worse).
The more sex is seen as distinct from simple procreation, the more human and less animal it becomes. Of course, sex can lead to good things and
bad things, as can happen whenever there is freedom—I've been saying this almost since the beginning.

All this fuss about the "immorality" of sex
stems from one of the most secret and hidden of
human fears: *the fear of pleasure*. And since sexual
pleasure is among the most intense and vivid we
can feel, it inevitably attracts distrust and wariness. What is so upsetting about pleasure? The
power, I imagine, that it has to please us so much.
Across the centuries, societies have always tried to
prevent their members from becoming addicted to
the pleasures of sex and so forgetting about work,

or defense, or the future. The truth is that nobody feels as at peace and at one with life as they do from sexual satisfaction, but if sex were to obliterate everything else from our minds, we would not survive. Human existence has always been dangerous; this was true for the first tribes that huddled around a fire millions of years ago, and is true for us today when we cross the street to buy a newspaper. Pleasure at times claims our attention so much that it could be dangerous to us, and so pleasure has always been beset by taboos and restraints, or carefully rationed, or allowed only on certain days, and so on. These are social precautions, taken so that nobody becomes too distracted from the dangers of living, that have often persisted for much longer than needed.

There are also people whose greatest pleasure seems to come from depriving others of pleasure. They are so afraid that pleasure will prove irresistible, they live in such dread of the consequences if one day they should give themselves over to pleasure, that they turn into professional denouncers of pleasures. It's sex here, food and drink there, gambling over there—all these fun and games with the world in such a sad state. Anything can come to be seen as bad or be used for bad purposes, but *nothing is bad just because practicing it gives pleasure.* Those professional denouncers of pleasure are called "puritans." A puritan believes that the sign that something is good lies in the fact that we don't like doing it. A puritan maintains that it is always better to suffer than to take pleasure (whereas in reality it is better to enjoy things well than suffer badly). Worst of all, a puritan believes that when someone is living well, things are going badly for him, and when someone is suffering it is because he is living right. Of course, puritans consider themselves the most moral of people, moral guardians of all their fellows. I don't want to exaggerate, but I consider any ordinary person more decent and moral than any official puritan. For a perfect example, let's take the woman who called the police to complain that some boys were swimming in the nude in front of her house. The police moved the boys on, but the woman called again to report that they were swimming farther up the beach, once again in the nude. Again, the police moved them on, and again the woman called to complain. "Lady," said the police inspector, "we moved them about a mile from your house." And she replied, with righteous puritan indignation, "That may be, but I can still see them through my binoculars."

Since to me puritanism is about as opposite as can be to an ethical view of life, you will never hear from me one word against pleasure, nor will I ever try to make you feel guilty, even marginally, over the urge to enjoy everything as much as possible, body and soul. I also want to pass on to you the advice of a wise old Frenchman whose works I highly recommend, Michel de Montaigne: "We must hang on tooth and nail to all the pleasures we take in life, for the years take them from us one after the other." I want to point out two things in Montaigne's maxim. He says that since time takes from us the possibilities of pleasure, it is not wise to wait too long to enjoy them. If you wait to take your pleasure, time will take pleasure from you. You must learn how to savor intelligently the joys of the present, as in the Latin tag *carpe diem*—seize the day. That doesn't mean that this very day you have to chase after all possible pleasure, but rather that you should *take pleasure in the day*. One of the surest ways of ruining your enjoyment of the present is to insist on having *everything*, every kind of odd and improbable satisfaction. Rather than becoming obsessed with pursuing every passing pleasure, try instead to find inklings of pleasure in everything you come across.

Which brings me back to Montaigne, when he talks about hanging on tooth and nail to all the pleasures we take in life. Taking pleasure, making good use of pleasure, means always having a certain control over it to keep it from shutting out other elements in your personal life. Some pages back, we spoke of the complexity of life, and how, to live it well, we should be careful not to oversimplify it. Pleasure is beguiling; it has a dangerous tendency to take over. If you give yourself over to it entirely, it can leave you with a sense of nothing more than having passed the time well. In taking pleasure, in making use of pleasure, try not to allow any single pleasure to distract you from all the others, or to obscure the whole context of your life. That is precisely the difference between "use" and "abuse": When you use pleasure well, you enrich your sense of being alive, and not just the pleasure itself but your whole life is more pleasing to you. When you realize that pleasure is taking over your life, that you are less interested in your life than in pleasure alone, then you are abusing pleasure and turning it into a refuge, somewhere to hide, somewhere to complain from, an escape from your existence.

Sometimes we say we are "dying of pleasure." Intense pleasure has the beneficial effect of dissolving the whole scaffolding of fears, routines, and trivialities that encompasses us and that often sours us rather than protects us. Losing all those protective shells, the self we habitually wear seems to die; later we are reborn, restored in strength and spirit. The French, specialists in these matters, refer to the orgasm as "the little death." It is a death that is life-giving, that makes us more aware, gentler, or more enthusiastic. In other cases, however, the pleasure we attain may kill us, quite literally. It may endanger our health, our body, or it may savage us by destroying our humanity, our concern for others, and all other things in our life. I won't deny that there are certain pleasures that seem worth risking your life for. The will to survive is all very well, but it is an instinct, and we humans do not live by instinct

alone. If we did, our lives would have little charm.
From a medical and professional point of view,
certain pleasures harm us and are dangerous, even
although they may seem perfectly respectable to a
less clinical view. Distrust those pleasures whose
principal attraction seems to lie in their danger. It
is one thing to "die of pleasure," and quite another when the pleasure involves dying or at least
risking death. When a pleasure kills you, or seems
on the point of killing you, or is killing in you all
that is human (all that makes your existence rich
and complex, and enables you to put yourself in
others' places), it is punishment disguised as pleasure, another deception practiced by our old enemy, death. Ethics means deciding always that life
is worth the trouble, that even the troubles we
have in life are worth the trouble; and they are
worth the trouble because it is through them that
we can attain our pleasures, which are always on
the other side of pain. So if you ask me to choose
between the pain of life and the pleasures of

death, I pick the first, since what I want is to live. I'm not interested in pleasures that allow me to escape from life; I'm interested only in ones that make it more intense and pleasurable.

Now here comes the big question: What is it that gives us the greatest gratification in life? What is the highest reward we can expect—from an effort, a caress, a word, a piece of music, an understanding, a machine, mountains of money, prestige, glory, power, love, ethics, anything you can think of? The answer, I warn you, is so simple as to seem deceptive: It is *the experience of joy.* Joy brings a justification to everything, and anything that separates us from feeling joy is misguided, misleading. What exactly is joy? It is a spontaneous Yes to life that springs up from inside, sometimes when we least expect it. It is an affirmation of what we are, or rather, of what we *feel* we are. Whoever feels joy has gained the greatest reward and lacks nothing. Those who never feel joy, however wise or handsome or healthy or rich or powerful or saintly they may be, lack what matters most, poor things. So, note this: Pleasure is most desirable when we know how to make it serve our joy in life, not when it confuses or compromises us. The negative side of pleasure is not suffering or even death; it is the absence of joy. When we begin not to feel joy in a pleasurable pursuit, then most certainly we are pursuing something that does not suit us. Joy, if you can understand me, is an experience that embraces pleasure and pain, death and life, an experience that accepts them once and for all.

The art of putting pleasure in the service of joy, the good sense that keeps pleasure from turning to disgust, has been called, from time immemorial, *temperance*. It is a fundamental ability among those who are not too fashionable nowadays: The who would replace it with a radical abstinence or a policelike prohibition. Before even trying to use well something that can be used badly (that is, abused), robot-minded people prefer to give it up completely and, if possible, have it banned by an outside authority, so that it does not depend on their will. They distrust everything that gives pleasure, or, even worse, they think that pleasure comes from what disgusts them. "Don't let me near that casino—I'll lose everything!" "Don't pass me that joint—it'll turn me into a gibbering addict!" They are like those who buy a machine to massage their stomach muscles to save them doing exercises. And of course, the more ruthlessly they deprive themselves of things, the more tantalizing these things become to them, the more they surrender to them with a bad conscience, dominated by the saddest of all pleasures, the pleasure of feeling guilty. Make no mistake about this: When someone enjoys feeling guilty, and thinks that things give more pleasure if they are forbidden or illegal, what that person is crying out for is *punishment*. The world is full of so-called rebels, who want only to be punished for being free and who hope for some superior power from this world or another to free them from their imprisonment to temptation.

Temperance on the other hand is an intelligent friendship with all things that give us pleasure. If someone says to you that pleasures are egoistical, since while you enjoy them someone else is always suffering, tell him that while it is good to help relieve the sufferings of others where possible, it is unhealthy to feel remorse over not suffering along with them or from taking pleasure as they would wish to. Understanding suffering and trying to relieve it assumes no more than a wish to have those who suffer also find pleasure; it does not mean that you must feel shame or guilt over taking your own pleasure. Only someone soured on life and bent on embittering it for others could come to believe that pleasure can be taken only at the expense of someone else. And if you come across someone who refers to pleasures as "dirty" or "animal," pleasures he does not dare to indulge in, you have my permission to look on him as dirty and as something of an animal himself. But enough of these questions for now, right?

Selections for Further Reading

What the ear wishes to hear is music, and anything that prevents us from hearing music we call an obstruction to hearing. What the eye desires is to look on beauty and what prevents us from looking on beauty we call an obstruction to sight. What the nose desires is to detect perfumes, and anything that prevents that we refer to as an obstruction to our sense of smell. What the mouth wishes is to speak of the just and the unjust, and anything that prevents us so speaking we call an obstruction to our understanding. What the body desires is to enjoy rich food and fine clothes, and anything that prevents such enjoyment we call an obstruction to bodily sensations. What the mind wishes is to be free, and anything that impedes that freedom we call an obstruction to our very nature.

—YANG CHU

Vice is a better corrective than virtue. Suffer a depraved person and you will have a horror of vice. Suffer a virtuous person and very soon you will hate all virtue.

—TONY DUVERT, *A Malevolent Alphabet*

Moderation presupposes pleasure, abstinence does not. Hence there are more abstainers than moderates.

—GEORG CHRISTOPH LICHTENBERG, *Aphorisms*

The only freedom which deserves the name, is that of pursuing our own good in our own way, so long as we do not attempt to deprive others of theirs, or impede their efforts to obtain it. Each is the proper guardian of his own health, whether bodily, *or* mental and spiritual. Mankind are greater gainers by suffering each other to live as seems good to themselves, than by compelling each to live as seems good to the rest.

—JOHN STUART MILL, *On Liberty*

General
Elections

O N ALL SIDES you'll hear it, so we have to bring it up and speak of it: Politics is scandalous, immoral! Politicians have no ethical standards! You've already heard these things hundreds of times. As a first rule, in all the matters we have been discussing it is wisest to distrust those who consider it their sacred duty to come down heavily on people in general, be they politicians, women, Jews, pharmacists, or people plain and simple, all lumped together. Ethics, as we have already said, is not an aggressive weapon, not an explosive for blowing up your neighbor and destroying his self-esteem, much less your neighbors in general, as if we had all been turned out in an endless stream, like doughnuts. What ethics is good for is to improve yourself, not to become an eloquent judge of your neighbor; and one thing ethics is fully aware of is that our neighbors— you, me, everyone else—are made by hand, as it were, one by one, with a pleasing difference. So when you hear someone begin to complain, "All [politicians, blacks, capitalists, Australians, firemen, whatever] are immoral, they don't have a scrap of ethical feelings," you can reply quietly, "Just be accountable for yourself, that's what matters."

Why, then, are politicians so badly thought of? After all, in a democracy we are all politicians, directly or indirectly. Most likely it is because the politicians we vote for are very much like ourselves—perhaps too much so. If they were very different from us (either much worse or obviously superior), then we wouldn't elect them to govern us. Only those who come to power without having to be elected (dictators, religious leaders, or kings) base their prestige on what is *different* about them, different from other people. Because they are distinct from others—through their power, through divine assistance, through family connection, whatever—they claim their right to rule without submitting themselves to a vote, or listening to the opinions of other citizens. Their grave advisers will tell them the "real people" support them, that those in the street are so enthusiastically on their side that there is no need to take a count to see how many they are. Those who wish to be *elected* to power, on the other hand, try to present themselves as "regular" human beings, human above all, with the same attachments, the same problems, and even the same small vices as the majority of people whose vote they need. They do of course offer ideas to better the lot of society, and present themselves as capable of turning these ideas into reality, but these are ideas everybody thinks about and discusses.

They must also always accept the possibility that they will be replaced in their posts if they are not as competent as they claimed to be, or as honest as they seemed. Among politicians, there are fine people, ruthless people, and opportunists, just as there are among firemen, professors, tailors, football players, any working group. So where does it come from, this bad reputation politicians have?

In the first place, politicians are extremely *visible* to human society; and they are also privileged. Their shortcomings are more public than those of other people, and besides, they face more opportunities for incurring abuse, strong or mild, than do other citizens. Nor does the fact that they are well-known, envied, and even feared lead to their being equally treated. Egalitarian societies, that is to say, democratic societies, show very little mercy to those who rise above the norm or fall below it. They love to shoot down outstanding people, and to wipe their feet on those who fall. Again, politicians are always ready to promise more things than they could or would wish to fulfill. Their constituents insist on it: A candidate who did not inflate the possibilities of the future to the electorate, who dwelt more on difficulties than on hopes, would soon find himself isolated. We convince ourselves that politicians have superhuman powers, and later on we do not forgive this inevitable deception. Altogether, it is better that politicians be ordinary people, dimwits, or even rowdies, much as we are, so that we are able to criticize them, control them, and drop them at a certain point. Their downfall comes when they see themselves as chiefs, feeling that they alone are always in full possession of the truth. The only way to retire them then is by force.

Let us leave our poor politicians in peace— they create enough uproar without any help from us. What matters to us now is to find out just what ethics and politics have to do with one another. They seem to have the same parentage— don't they both talk of *living well*? Ethics is the art of choosing what suits us and living as well as we can. Politics sets out to do everything it can for the convenience of society, in such a way that individuals can choose what suits them. As nobody lives alone (and I have said to you that the connections you make with your fellow humans are at the heart of life), anyone concerned with the ethics of living well cannot pretend to an Olympian detachment from politics. It would be like making yourself comfortable in a house without wanting to know anything about the drips, the rats, the temperamental heater, and the wormy cement.

There are, however, important differences between ethics and politics. Ethics concerns itself with how an individual person (you, me, anyone) acts with respect to his freedom, while politics tries to coordinate what many people do with their freedom in a way that will be beneficial to all. In ethics, it is important to *want* well, because ethics is mostly about what each person does because he or she wants to—not about what happens to us, or what we do because we have to. In politics, on the other hand, what matters are the *results* of actions, and the politician will press with all the means at his disposal, including force, to obtain certain results and to avoid others. Let's take a simple case: obeying traffic lights. From the moral point of view, the positive attitude is to respect the light (understanding its general use, putting yourself in the place of others who could be hurt if you disobey); but if you look at it politically, what matters is that nobody jumps the light, even if they obey only through fear of a fine or prison. To politicians, all those who obey the red light are equally "good," whether they obey from fear, habit, or superstition, or from rational conviction; but from an ethical point of view, these last are the only "good" ones, since they have a better understanding of the use of freedom. In a word, there is a difference between the ethical question I put to myself (how do I choose to act with respect to others?) and the preoccupation of politics, namely that the majority should live their lives in the most satisfactory and harmonious manner.

Pay no attention to those who tell you that the world, politically, is unlivable, that nobody can attain a good life, ethically speaking, in a context as unjust, as violent, and as aberrant as the one we live in. The same thing has been said in every age, and with justification, for human societies have always been of this world, and hence full of flaws, abuses, and crimes. Yet in every age there have been people capable of living well, or at least of trying to live well. When they can, they help to improve the society through what they are able to accomplish; if that is not possible, at least they don't make it worse, which is no small thing. They have fought—and they still fight, you can be sure—for the human relations within politics to be simply that, more human, or if you like, less violent and more just; but they have never imagined that everything in the world would become perfect and human. Circumstances may not allow them to live a life that is any more than relatively good, worse than they would wish. Yet, however adverse the circumstances, we one and all still bear the responsibility for our own acts; other people are only excuses. In the same way, to envision a utopia, a political order so flawless that in it everyone is automatically good, since wrongdoing is not permitted, is tantamount to putting our heads in the sand. In spite of all the wrongdoing in the world, there have always been those who did good things because they wished to; but also, in spite of all the things we have brought about for the general good, the bad will always seem to triumph to one who wishes it so. This is what we called freedom a short time ago, you remember?

From an ethical point of view, from the perspective of what is suitable to the good life, what kind of political organization is to be preferred? Which one is worth achieving and maintaining? If you cast your mind back over what we have been saying up until now, certain aspects of that ideal will be clear to you:

■ Since all ethics stems from freedom, without which there is no worthwhile life, our political system must always make maximal allowance for, or put minimal restraints on, public manifestations of human freedom: freedom to meet with, and separate from, others; freedom to express opinions; freedom to invent, in art and science; freedom to do work that fits well; freedom to be involved in public matters; freedom to move and to settle; freedom to enjoy what we want, in body or in spirit. It must also abjure dictates of any kind, particularly those made "for our own good" or "for the good of all." What is best for us, in particular and in general, is to be free. Of course, a political regime that gives freedom its proper place also insists on the *social responsibility* of each person's actions and omissions (I say "omissions" because sometimes not doing is a form of action). In political systems where individuals are not held responsible, neither as a rule are their governments, which are always acting out of "historical necessity" or the imperatives of "reasons of state." Watch out for politicians who see everyone as a victim of circumstances, or even as the cause of them!

■ A basic principle of the good life is to treat other people as people: to be able to put ourselves in the place of our fellows and alter our interests to fit in with theirs. Put another way, it is trying to take on the interests of another person as if they were your own, and your own as if they were someone else's. This is what is called *justice*, and there can be no respectable political regime that does not claim, through its laws and institutions, to disseminate justice among all members of society. The condition that human beings demand of one another—that they all be treated the same, whatever their sex, their skin color, their ideas, their preferences—is called *dignity*. And notice this strange thing: Although dignity is what all human beings have in common, it is precisely what marks them out as recognizable, unique, and unrepeatable. *Things* can be interchanged, one with another; similar or better things can be substituted for other things—in a word, things have their "price." Money makes these interchanges easy, since it measures them all on a uniform scale. Every human being has dignity and no price, that is, he cannot be replaced, and should not be mistreated for the benefit of another. When I say he cannot be replaced, I am not referring to what he does—one carpenter can do the work of another carpenter. I am referring to his own self, his personality, what he truly is. When I talk of "mistreating" someone, I mean that not even if he is punished in accordance with the law, not even if he is a political enemy, should he ever be denied consideration and respect. Even in war, which represents the greatest possible fail-

ure of the "good life," there are certain acts that
are seen as crimes even worse than the organized
crime that war represents. Human dignity asks
that we treat all our fellow human beings justly,
for that treatment demonstrates that each person
is unique and irreplaceable, with the same right to
social recognition as anyone else.

■ Experience reveals even to the most fortunate
of us the reality of human suffering. To take
someone else in all seriousness, to put ourselves
in his place, we must not only recognize his dignity as a fellow human but also have sympathy for
his pain, for the misfortunes that through his own
fault or through accident or biological necessity
afflict him, as sooner or later they can afflict us all
—misfortunes like illness, age, insurmountable
disability, abandonment, emotional or mental dis-
tress, loss of a loved one or of something irreplaceable, threats or violent encounters with
stronger or less scrupulous forces. A desirable
political community must guarantee assistance

from the community within the limits of the possible for those who suffer, and help those who for some reason cannot help themselves. The difficulty is in providing this help without limiting the freedom and dignity of the person in need. Sometimes, the state, on the pretext of helping sick people, ends up by treating the whole population as if it were sick. Misfortune puts us in the hands of others, and extends the collective power over the individual.

Whoever wishes to live a good life in accordance with ethical standards must also want the political community to be based on freedom, justice, and assistance where required. Over the last two centuries, modern democracy has tried to set up, first in theory, then little by little in practice, those minimal ethical obligations in society. They are what we call *human rights*, which to our collective shame remain today a catalog of worthy aims rather than of effective achievements. To press to achieve them all in their entirety, everywhere and for everyone, not just for some and some alone, is still the single political end from which ethics can never detach itself. As to choosing what you are going to wear on your lapel from among the labels that say "left," "right," "center," or whatever, let's just leave these all behind us.

What seems obvious to me is that many of the problems we face today ("we" meaning the five billion of us at present crowding the planet and increasing, according to the census) cannot be resolved or even formulated except in global terms. Think of hunger, which still causes the deaths of so many millions, or the economic or educational backwardness of many countries, or the prevalence of brutal political systems that oppress their people without mercy and threaten neighboring countries, or the squandering of money and knowledge in manufacturing arms, or the plain and simple misery of too many people, even in rich countries. I think that the present political fragmentation of a world already unified by economic interdependence and a universal system of communications does no more than perpetuate these evils and doom all proposed solutions. Consider the insane investment in armaments of funds that could take care of most of the world's current wants; and military aggression, the immoral art of suppressing others instead of giving them proper consideration as fellow human beings. Do you think there is any way of putting an end to that madness other than by setting up a world authority with enough force behind it to dissuade any country from embarking on acts of aggression? I said to you earlier that some things cannot be replaced. This thing on which we live, the planet Earth, with its animal and vegetable life in delicate equilibrium, is more than anything irreplaceable: If from lust for profit or from stupidity we destroy it, we can't simply "buy" another. Our Earth is not a jumble of small patches and separate pieces. The task of maintaining it as both habitable and well cared for can be taken on only by people who see themselves as a world community, not by groups who myopically pursue their own advantage.

To organize human beings as human beings and not as members of a particular tribe seems to me to be of the first political importance. The diversity of our life forms is essential to us— imagine how tedious our lives would be without diversity—but there must always be a basic tolerance among them, and certain situations demand a common effort. Otherwise, all we would arrive at would be a diversity not of culture but of crime. I confess that I hate all doctrines that pit certain people irresolvably against others: *racism*, which classifies people as first, second, or third class according to pseudoscientific fantasies; *nationalism*, the ferocious kind that sees the individual as nothing and the collective identity as everything; *ideologies* of the fanatical kind, religious or secular, that are unable to accept any peaceful differences of opinion and demand that the whole world recognize and believe in what they have decided is the only truth. But I don't want at this point to beat you over the head with politics, or tell you my views on the divine and the human. In this last chapter I have tried to show you that there are political exigencies that nobody who wishes to live well can refuse to face. As for all the other things, we will get to them in time. In another book.

Selections for Further Reading

Not Man but men inhabit this planet. Plurality is the law of the earth.

—HANNAH ARENDT, *The Life of the Spirit*

If I knew something that was useful to me but prejudicial to my family, I would drive it from my mind. If I knew something useful to my family but not to my country, I would try to forget it. If I knew something useful to my country but prejudicial to Europe, or useful to Europe but prejudicial to mankind, I would look on it as something criminal, because I am of necessity a man, while I am a Frenchman only by accident.

—MONTESQUIEU

The Utopians think it a bad idea to make treaties at all, even if they are faithfully kept. The treaty implies that men divided by some natural obstacle as slight as a hill or a brook are joined by no bond of nature; it assumes that they are born rivals and enemies, and are right in trying to destroy one another except when a treaty restrains them. Beside, they see that treaties do not really promote friendship; for both parties still retain the right to prey on one another, unless extreme care has been used in drafting the treaty to outlaw freebooting. The Utopians think, on the other hand, that no man should be considered an enemy who has done no harm, that the kinship of nature is as good as a treaty, and that men are united more firmly by good will than by pacts, by their hearts than by their words.

—THOMAS MORE, *Utopia*

Epilogue

You'll Have to Think About It

Well, that's it. In spite of all the obstacles, of course, but the main things I think have been said. I refer to the "main things" I am able to tell you for the moment; other, much more "main" things you will have to pick up from others or, even better, think out for yourself. I don't ask you to take this book too seriously—it's very possible that it's not a real book of ethics, if Wittgenstein is right. That most distinguished of modern philosophers thought it so utterly impossible to write a true book on ethics that he declared, "If a man could write a book on ethics that were truly a book about ethics, that book would blow

up at a stroke all other books in the world."
Here I am, finishing up this book I wrote for you
without hearing any annihilating rumble. My own
worn books, which I love so much, are still standing safely on my library shelves. Obviously, I
haven't come up with the magic words, *the* book
of ethics. You can relax. Many others have tried
before with books that did not blow the rest of
literature to smithereens but that are well worth
your getting to know: Aristotle, Spinoza, Kant,
Nietzsche. Although I promised you not to quote
from them all the time, since we were talking
among friends, still I confess that the most appealing material in the previous pages comes from
them. I have merely fathered a few idiocies (no,
please, I don't mean you!).

So don't take this book too seriously, Amador,
because, among other things, seriousness is not as
a rule an unequivocal sign of wisdom, as serious
people believe. Intelligence must know how to
laugh. The book's theme, however, you would do

well not to pass over: It talks about what you can do with your life, and if that doesn't interest you then I don't know what will. How to live in the best possible way? That question is of far more substance to me than others that appear to be weightier, like, Does life have meaning? Is living worthwhile? Is there life after death? Look, life does have meaning, one single meaning: It goes forward. There is no video recorder, the plays are not repeated, and you cannot go back to correct anything. For that reason, you have to think deeply about what you want, and trust what you do. The meaning of life? First, try not to fail; then, try to fail without falling apart. As for whether living is worthwhile, I pass on to you the answer given by Samuel Butler, an English writer fond of irony: "That's a question for an embryo, not a man." Whatever criteria you choose in deciding whether life is worth living, you are taking them from the very life in which you are presently occupied. Also, if you reject life, you do it in the name of living values, the ideals and illusions you have absorbed during the business of living. It is life that is of value, even to the person who comes to the conclusion that it is not worth living. It would make more sense to ask ourselves questions like, Does death have meaning? Is death worthwhile? because we know nothing of that, since what we do know and consider worthwhile all comes from life! I will dare to say even more, now that nobody is listening, that the good man ought also to feel an active antipathy toward death. Note: I say "antipathy" and not "fear." Fear always has an air of respect about it, and is somewhat submissive. I don't think death deserves that. What interests me is not that there be life after death, but that there be life *before* death, and that that life be good, not just a matter of surviving, or a constant fear of dying.

So we are left again with the question of how to live better. In the previous chapters I have tried

not so much to answer it as to make you understand it more deeply. As for the answer, I'm afraid
there's nothing for it but for you to find it person-
ally. For three reasons:

- Because of the very incompetence of
your teacher, me. How can I teach anyone
to live well if I only manage to live normally
and am grateful for it? I feel like a bald man
advertising an infallible hair restorer.
- Because living is not an exact science
like mathematics, like music. You can learn
certain laws of music and you can listen to
the works of great composers, but if you
don't have a good ear, a sense of rhythm,
and a voice, they will be of little use to you.
The same is true of the art of living: What
can be demonstrated falls very well on someone who is ready for it, but to someone who
is "deaf" by nature, it will be boring, or will
confuse him even more. Of course, in this

area, the majority of those who are "deaf"
usually are so by their own volition.

■ The good life is not a general idea,
turned out on an assembly line, but something that is made to individual measure-
ments. Each of us must go on discovering
it according to our individual natures—
unique, unrepeatable, and fragile. In living
well, the wisdom or the example of others
can be a help but cannot be a substitute.

Life is not like medicine, which always comes with
a paper explaining the side effects and the appropriate dosage. We get life with no prescription or
prospectus. Ethics cannot supply all these defi-
ciencies, because it is no more than the record of
things done by human beings to compensate for
them. A French writer who died recently,
Georges Perec, wrote a book called *Life: A User's
Manual*; it is a delightful and intelligent literary

joke, but not an ethical system. I have chosen not to give you a series of instructions on concrete questions such as abortion, contraception, or objections of conscience. Nor have I dared, as so many moralists do, to preach to you in a sorrowful or indignant tone about the "evils" of our century: about consumerism, about lack of common cause, about money-greed, about violence, about the crisis of values, oh, oh, oh! I have my own opinions on those matters and on others, but I am not the voice of ethics; I am your father, no more. For me, the only ethical precept I pass on to you is that you seek out and think for yourself, in full freedom, responsibly, with no tricks. I have tried to show you ways forward, but neither I nor anyone else can carry you. Can I finish with a last counsel? When it is a matter of choosing, try always to make those choices that will allow you the greatest number of possible options. Choose what opens things up for you, to other people, to new experiences, to a variety of joys. Avoid what encloses you and buries you. For the rest, good luck! And remember that other cry which a voice like mine passed to you in your dream when the whirlwind threatened to sweep you away: Keep your nerve! Have confidence in yourself!

Farewell

Goodbye, my friendly reader. Try not to use up your life in hating and being afraid.

—STENDHAL, *Lucien Leuwen*

Grateful acknowledgment is made to the following for use of selections included in this volume (except as noted, all translations are by Alastair Reid): Harcourt Brace and Company, selection from *The Other Voice* by Octavio Paz (copyright © 1990 by Editorial Seix-Barral, S.A., and Octavio Paz); HarperCollins Ltd., selection from *Mysticism and Logic* by Bertrand Russell (copyright 1929 by Bertrand Russell); Henry Holt and Company, selections from *Man for Himself: An Inquiry into the Psychology of Ethics* by Erich Fromm (copyright 1947 by Erich Fromm); Albert LaFarge, selections from Aristotle, Homer, and Seneca (translated by Albert LaFarge); W.W. Norton & Company, selections from *Utopia* by Thomas More, translated by Robert M. Adams (copyright © 1975 by W.W. Norton & Co.); Princeton University Press, selections from *The Collected Works of Spinoza*, Vol. I, translated by Edwin Curley (copyright © 1985 by Princeton University Press); and Charles Scribner's Sons, an imprint of Macmillan Publishing Company, selections from *I and Thou* by Martin Buber, translated by Walter Kaufman (translation copyright © 1970 by Charles Scribner's Sons).

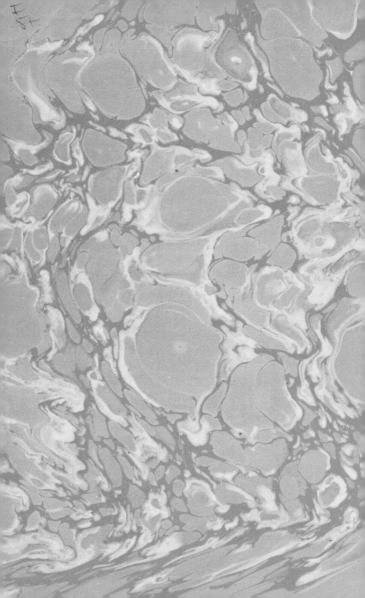